❖ GOD'S PLAGIARIST

❖   R. HOWARD BLOCH

₽ GOD'S
LAGIARIST

Being an Account of

the Fabulous Industry

and Irregular Commerce

of the Abbé Migne

The University of Chicago Press
Chicago and London

R. HOWARD BLOCH is professor of French at the University of California, Berkeley. He is a coeditor of the journal *Representations* and author of a novel entitled *Moses in the Promised Land* (1988). Among his scholarly works are *Etymologies and Genealogies* (1983), *The Scandal of the Fabliaux* (1986), and *Medieval Misogyny and the Invention of Western Romantic Love* (1991), all published by the University of Chicago Press.

The University of Chicago Press, Chicago 60637
The University of Chicago Press, Ltd., London
© 1994 by the University of Chicago
All rights reserved. Published 1994
Printed in the United States of America
02 01 00 99 98 97 96 95 94   1 2 3 4 5
ISBN: 0-226-05970-7 (cloth)

Library of Congress Cataloging-in-Publication Data

Bloch, R. Howard.
   God's plagiarist : being an account of the fabulous industry and irregular commerce of the abbé Migne / R. Howard Bloch.
     p.   cm.
   Includes bibliographical references and index.
   1. Migne, J.-P. (Jacques-Paul), 1800–1875. 2. Catholic literature—Publication and distribution—France—History—19th century. 3. Christian literature, Early—Publication and distribution—France—History—19th century. 4. Plagiarism—France—History—20th century. I. Title.
   Z305.M46B57   1994
   381'.45002'0944—dc20
                                  93-31872
                                      CIP

To the memory of Leo Lowenthal, 1900–1993, who
understood the relation between a life of the mind
and drygoods.

❖ CONTENTS

❖ ACKNOWLEDGMENTS

I would like to thank Jesse Gellrich, who originally put me on the track of Migne; Katherine Streip, who read the typescript with an eye that would have impressed even Migne's proofers; and Jennifer Looper, who prepared the index. I am also grateful to the American Council of Learned Societies, the Dean of International and Area Studies at University of California, Berkeley, and the University of California Humanities Research Fellowship Committee for affording me delicious time in the Bibliothèque nationale and Archives nationales, Paris.

❖ 1

The Abbé and the Police

Migne Martyr

I ALWAYS WONDERED how he did it. The average American academic publishes two books in a lifetime—one for tenure, the other for promotion to the rank of full professor. The abbé Jacques-Paul Migne published a book every ten days for thirty years. And he did it, like some Balzacian self-made man who could have been his contemporary, practically without money. Migne arrived in Paris almost penniless in the early 1830s and with only a meager education. In the space of a decade he had created what Ambroise Firmin Didot would refer to as "the greatest publishing enterprise since the invention of printing"—the Ateliers catholiques of Montrouge, worth over 3,000,000 francs at the time of his death.

Migne is best known, of course, for the *Patrologia Latina*, in 217 tomes and 218 volumes, issued in two series between 1844 and 1855, and for the *Patrologia Graeca*, which appeared in a Greco-Latin edition (161 tomes in 166 volumes) between 1857 and 1866, as well as for an edition of the Greek Fathers in Latin only, 81 tomes in 85 volumes. The patrologies combined weigh in at over a million pages. Yet they represent only about one-half of his total output. Migne had published approximately 400 books before the first page of the patrologies had even gone to print. The entire corpus, comprised under the general rubric of the *Bibliothèque universelle du clergé*, includes the: 1) *Scripturae sacrae cursus completus* (25 volumes, 1838–40); 2) *Theologia cursus completus* (25 volumes, 1840–42); 3) *Démonstrations évangeliques des plus célèbres défenseurs du Christianisme* (18 volumes, 1842–43); 4) *Orateurs sacrés*, in two series (66 and 33 volumes, 1844–66); 5) series of theological encyclopedias, the *Première encyclopédie théologique ou série de dictionnaires sur toutes les parties de la science religieuse* (50 volumes, 1844–52), *Nouvelle encyclopédie théologique* (53 volumes, 1851–59), *Troisième et dernière encyclopédie*

1

ecclésiastique (66 volumes, 1851–59); 6) *Cours complet d'histoire ecclésiastique* (27 volumes, 1862–); 7) *Summa aurea de laudibus B. Mariae virginis* (13 volumes, 1866–); 8) 150 diverse volumes published between 1840 and 1868.[1]

Unless we assume that Migne read between fifty and one hundred pages of Latin or Greek each day, in addition to the fifty to one hundred pages he published a day, we can conclude that one simple answer to the question of how he did as much as he did lies in the simple fact that Migne did not read, could not have read, as much as he wrote—or at least as much as he edited. Indeed, questioned by the authorities about an article that had appeared in one of the ten newspapers he also owned and managed in the same thirty-year period, Migne defended himself before the Ministre de l'Intérieur by claiming not to have read even a tenth of what he had published.[2] Even at that his days were full. Migne is alleged to have worked sixteen hours a day, reserving, as the top of the letterhead on some of his stationery asserts, the hour of 1 p.m. to 2 p.m. for visits, and never, by his own account, taking recreation, not even one hour a year.[3] "The more we work the better off and the happier we are," Migne writes to Dom Pitra, the man most responsible for the general plan as well for as the editorial execution of the patrologies. As abstemious where food was concerned as he was with time, Migne lived like a monk: "in order to preserve the freedom of our spirit, we do not eat more than a simple seminarian or a worker."[4] His friend and publicist, A. Bonnetty, editor of the *Annales de philosophie chrétienne,* insists upon the rigors of Migne's task, a race from the start of brute human endurance against time: "It is part of the duty of the Bishops, the leaders of seminaries, curés who love religion, to come to his assistance, and it is necessary to do so as soon as possible; for, humanly speaking, one man alone cannot bear for very long such a heavy burden."[5]

Migne's denial of the flesh was also characterological. For if he appears by any standard to be what today would pass for a workaholic, it is because persistence, a stubbornness associated in the folklore of French regional identities with the Auvergne from which he came, was so profound a trait of personality that in everything having to do with the patrologies, he is reputed never to have relinquished any point. Dom Pitra, complaining to the famous Dom Guéranger (March 20, 1844) of Migne's extravagance, recounts the story of his heroic struggle over the very epic title of the *Cours complets*:

. . . an excessive title, one that he wants to display like a poster at the beginning of his patrologie, a whole page in-folio of tightly packed lines in which are repeated ad nauseam how complete, how perfect, how uniformly printed, how economical, and then still more impossible promises, a display of which makes him look like a salesman of suspicious goods. I tried to cut all that with bloody notes ("des apostilles sanglantes"), and I insisted upon the removal of the whole thing. This is where the matter stands for the last three days, he is not moving . . . I hope he will give in.[6]

Migne himself was so energetically tenacious in every aspect of the production and distribution of the patrologies, so resolutely attentive to every detail, so painstakingly precise in his accounts, that he vows in a letter of February 10, 1852, to the Ministre de l'Instruction Publique et des Cultes de Paris to pursue a delinquent debtor, a fellow priest whom the Bishop of Algiers has let out of his sight and who owes him 190 francs for thirty volumes of the *Cours d'orateurs*, "even as far as California."[7] Migne not only lived like a monk, working every hour and in the mortification of his own flesh, but he demonstrated something akin to the iron will of the early Christian martyrs.

To say that Migne seems to have sacrificed himself materially, even bodily, to his publications is not to suggest that his own sense of mission abounded in humility. Indeed, neither immune to financial matters nor insensitive to the fact that one of his detractors has represented him to the Pope as a "speculator," he refers explicitly to his "life of a martyr" in which, he affirms, even more intense pain will not cause him to waver.[8] Where the patrologies are concerned, Migne compares favorably the 240 tables of "our new and truly monumental edition" of the Fathers to the twelve tasks of Hercules, who presumably possessed neither more will nor more force than the abbé himself and for whom the financial expenditure was certainly less. "The most extraordinary thing in the world since one invented the book, that which surpasses even the 12 tasks of Hercules, are the 240 Index Tables [of the patrologies] which took 49 editors 500 men-years of time, and which cost the editor in chief more than half a million francs."[9] The publication of the patrologies, "the most colossal enterprise of our century," is, Migne maintains, a greater accomplishment than the tunnel blasted through Mont Cenis, greater even than the construction of ten cathedrals.[10]

Elsewhere, Migne pictures himself as a medieval monk staving off the barbarians in what were the new invasions and threat to the Church of the century following the French Revolution. Contemporaries saw him thus: "He has undertaken, in our time, that which the monks of the middle ages did in order to save from destruction the writings of the Fathers of the Church as well as pagan writers," writes Cardinal Bonald, Archbishop of Lyon (Archives Nationales F18 369). Those of the generation immediately succeeding that of Migne were no less eloquent. Witness the abbé Brémond:

Finally, like an imposing Titan, Migne appears, at the threshold of a gigantic forge; and all the pages of the Catholic encyclopedia are blown before him like autumn leaves swept away by the Mistral wind. Two hundred and thirty-one volumes of the Latin Patrologie, one hundred and sixty-one of the Greek Patrologie, and what volumes! God and lead, plaster and granite. If ever new barbarians invade, they will stop with terror before these colossal bricks; and they will recognize in this fantastic fortress the mark of the infernal gods.[11]

And Migne did all he did, Bonnetty insists, all alone, without the assistance of government or church, most of his subscribers being "foreigners, Protestants, or Greeks."[12]

Indeed, in the self-representation of his publishing venture Migne set out explicitly to rival the Protestants in England and Germany by publishing the Fathers of the Church. One of the numerous prospectuses published for publicity purposes recounts the visit of a Protestant from Oxford who confesses that "the excellent apology for the Church that he has just read would have converted him if he had not been converted already." Curious as to which book the Protestant referred to, Migne is greeted with an answer that could not have pleased him more had he written it himself (which, as we shall see, he probably did).

This book, he responded with a smile, is the work of the *Ateliers catholiques*. I do not judge the fruit by the tree, but the tree by the fruit; and many a Protestant who praises his religion because it produced Chambers's publishing house in Edinburgh, recognizes the vanity of his prejudice against the Catholic church in seeing how completely Migne's publishing house in Montrouge surpasses it in size, in efficiency, in piety, and in every other respect. I have been all over Europe, and I have no doubt that the principal means which God uses in order to further the interests of the Church in England, Germany, and Russia is precisely this turning toward the reading of the Fathers. For, can there be anyone who does not know that it was the study of the Fathers which produced Puseyism, the return of Newman, and the conversions that occur every day in England? Who could doubt that the only scholarly study worthy of rationalism, the only bridge between PROTESTANTISM and CATHOLICISM in Germany is also the study of the Holy Fathers? In Russia, it is the reading, the translation and the reprinting of these incomparable ancestors which prevents the Greeks, separated from the Church, from withdrawing entirely (AN F18 369).

In the nostalgic spirit of a Church reunited, Migne was convinced, or at least he tried to convince others, that purchase of the *Cursus completus* would undo the effects not only of the great schism, but of the Reformation as well.

Most of all, however, Migne aimed to reverse France's own revolution, something obvious in the scope implicit to the very title of his undertaking. In establishing a Universal Catholic Library, a *Bibliothèque universelle du clergé,* Migne envisaged more than merely making a multitude of books available. He sought in the period of greatest ecclesiastical depredation following the end of the Ancien Régime, to create a printing office that would surpass that of the Imprimerie nationale:

If you would like to see carried out all at once and on a grand scale all the arts relating to printing, you are invited to honor with your presence the *Ateliers catholiques* of Petit-Montrouge. They are all to be found there. Indeed, in order to be convinced of that, one need only take a look at the words *print shop, bookstore, foundry, stereotyping, glazing, smoothing, collating,* and *binding,* which are on the entrance to the establishment, and which cannot be found together elsewhere, not even in the Imprimerie nationale (AN F18 369).

And he sought to create a library that would surpass the Bibliothèque nationale: "It is, it appears to us, useless to say more in order to explain what we have done and in order to prove that the

Patrologie is henceforth the necessary foundation of any serious library," he writes in the *Annales de philosophie chrétienne* of 1864. "Even that of the *rue Richelieu* would not contain the elements necessary to constitute our *Cours* in its entirety."[13] What's more, in conceiving of such a library as universal, Migne hoped to undo the very conceptual foundation of the Revolution—the secular science of the Philosophes. The patrologies were intended from the start to rival the "funeste" *Encyclopédie* of d'Alembert and Diderot. "This encyclopedia, compared to the two *Patrologies* of the abbé Migne," writes Migne's publicist Bonnetty, "is a pygmy of science and utility."[14] His Herculean task almost complete, Migne himself asks rhetorically, "Of what use are all other literary works! Of what use the Encyclopedias of the 18th and 19th centuries! Of what use all other printed works! Mere children's games, of which the greatest is nothing compared to ours!" (*PL* 218, col. 1).

Migne had experienced directly the effects of the Revolution, and it is difficult not to see in several biographical events which supposedly occurred in the early days of the July Monarchy the motivating trauma that would, if not produce, at least influence the will to the patrologies. Migne had in 1825 been named curé at Puiseaux, chef-lieu de canton in the Gatinais—and a place, according to his earliest biographer, Hippolyte Barbier, filled with "the lowly shops and the little clerks in notary offices, that is, a liberalism of the kitchen sink." In one episode a fellow priest, evicted from his parish, was arrested at the entrance to town by the garde nationale. The secular authorities intended to hold him overnight when Migne arrived to "guarantee" his freedom. "We do not recognize even you," one of the guards is purported to have replied, "and you're quite lucky that your opposition to the laws is not punished." Migne is alleged to have encouraged the priest to lie down in what today would be considered an act of civil disobedience. When the guards then menaced him with their bayonets, he reportedly called their bluff: "Let's see if you will dare to push this ignoble joke to the point of murder?"[15]

In a second episode, which perhaps occurred in retaliation for the first but which was certainly more indicative of what was to come, Migne was denounced by the authorities for having shown insufficient respect for the tricolor flag placed on the altar of the church as a prank by "anti-clerical liberals" on the day of Fête-Dieu 1831. Explanations having been called for, Migne composed a two hundred page brochure analyzing the relation between church and state entitled *De la Liberté, par un Prêtre* (*On Freedom, by a Priest*), which Barbier claims to have read, and whose contents are, Barbier asserts, "no less provocative (piquant) than the title," but which never saw the light of day. For Migne was called before the Bishop of Orléans, Mgr de Beauregard, who confiscated it without having read "a single one of the lines he condemned."[16] The exchange is significant and indeed had a determining effect on what was to come. In it not only is the oppositional tenacity of Migne's character first made manifest, but the conflict with Mgr de Beauregard was directly responsible for Migne's decision to leave the provinces for Paris. Migne's resistance to the civil authorities as well as to the authority of bishops will later play itself out in terms of repeated confrontations with the Bishop of Paris and in the founding of a newspaper—*La Vérité canonique*—aimed in large part at advising priests who experience similar difficulties with the ecclesiastical hierarchy.

More important, Migne had until then been known primarily for his powers as an orator. "He is well endowed," Barbier tells us, "physically as well as morally with all the qualities which make for a true orator: large physique, large and nobly carried head, the look of an eagle which exhales nonetheless the most unctuous sensitivity, a limpid and sonorous voice, a forceful and colorful manner of speech, a rare capacity for improvisation" (p. 300). *De la Liberté, par un Prêtre,* in contrast, signals Migne's disappearance as a body, as a simple voice, and his entrance into writing—into excessive writing at that. For the very nature of his response offers a glimpse in embryo of his prodigious capacity for written production. It is as if the confrontation with Mgr de Beauregard were the traumatic event, the repressed wound, at the core of his being, for which the rest of Migne's career would compensate. Mgr de Beauregard's muzzling of Migne was for him the equivalent of a conversion, not toward belief in the mysteries of the Christian religion, but toward using the writing that had been suppressed in order to convert others; it contained the potential for discovery of a mission. "Migne could not tolerate defeat," his modern-day biographer A.-G. Hamman asserts, "and his revenge would consist in publishing whole libraries instead of a brochure."[17]

Migne's unresolved confrontation with the power of bishops never ceased to define his life's project. The muteness into which he had been forced can be seen on some fundamental level to have produced in him what some—especially Dom Pitra—considered to be an hysterical profusion of exorbitant writing: not only the *Bibliothèque universelle du clergé* but the extravagant brochures, the advertisements for himself printed as freestanding broad sheets, the self-glorifying reviews placed in the *Annales de philosophie chrétienne;* in short, what we shall see to be a plethora of compensatory self-promotions surrounding the patrologies. For even as his life's work was well on the way toward realization, Migne still dreamed, upon completion, of deferring to a higher authority, of having the last word—perhaps with Mgr de Beauregard—by presenting a copy to the Pope. "I am curious to know if the Holy Father knows of my existence," he wonders in a letter to Dom Pitra of 1864. "My well-established destiny, unless prevented by death, is to go to Rome as soon as I will have finished and to deposit myself a copy of all my great publications."[18] In the event that he should die before finishing, however, the wound of this founding editorial rejection might still be healed. The patrologies represented in Migne's emotional economy a means of salvation. "I am counting upon you for several of these *conspectus* (notices) to be carried out in my old age or while I will be serving in Purgatory," he writes to Dom Pitra on March 12, 1862, "if, all things being equal, my *cours complet de Patrologie* does not cause me to go directly to heaven."[19]

Migne Miles Christi

THAT MIGNE'S MOTIVATION in creating the *Bibliothèque universelle du clergé* was in part personal should not blind us to the historical context of his undertaking, which, together with his pastoral experience, produced an extraordinary conjunction of the moment and the man. Like the Garnier Frères, who installed themselves in the Palais-Royal toward 1833; Aristide Boucicaut, the transforming genius of "Le Bon Marché" (more later), who arrived from Normandy in 1835; and Pierre Larousse, who came to Paris in 1839, Migne followed a movement within France toward the capital. He found in Paris of the 1830s a world of powerful industrial and technological progress, especially within the realm of printing, a world in which what must have seemed like the intense capacities of capital to feed fantasies of ambition must have encouraged, again like so many characters invented by Balzac, who embarked upon his own printing venture in 1826 and who chronicles this world in *Illusions perdues* (1837), not only a sense of the feasibility of epic undertakings, but one of the infinite potential of the individual will in their realization. "Whatever happens, I have announced that I will carry out this project," he writes to Dom Guéranger. "Well, I will do it even if it takes all I possess."[20]

From the outset Migne was convinced that, through sheer determination and force of character, anything was possible for the energetic individual at mid-century:

Have no illusions about my mission [he writes to the journalist Louis Veuillot]. I am neither a saint nor a learned man; but by the sheer force of my character, I believe that I will render to the Church the greatest service that has ever been rendered, and I hope to die as the priest who will have done it the greatest service in the world by reviving in toto its tradition.[21]

Migne's early adventure as a curé, thus seen in the context of potential recovery of that which the Revolution had taken away, a personal wound and a more general one, induced a heightened awareness of his historical mission. Yet the abbé's iron will only takes us part of the way toward an answer to the question posed at the outset of how any one individual could have done as much as he did, ambition itself having been catalyzed by historical conditions beyond its reach—not only the heady atmosphere of economic and social expansion, but that of the Catholic renewal of the post-Napoleonic era.

It is, of course, unthinkable within the present context to attempt to retrace the history of the Church in the period from Migne's installation in Puiseaux in 1825 to his death in Paris half a century later. Yet, in most general terms, the devastation of the decades immediately following the Revolution entailed the closing

of abbeys and places of worship (a number of which were retrofit-
ted to serve the military), the alienation of ecclesiastical property
and revenues, the dispersal of teaching institutions and libraries,
the dissolution of whole religious orders, the abdication of a large
number of priests along with the gradual attrition of an aging
clergy. In 1814 9 episcopal seats were vacant, and 34 bishops were
older than sixty. Between 1801 and 1814 approximately 6,000
priests were ordained as against 6,848 deaths between 1806 and
1814. As many as 3,345 parishes remained without local pastoral
care.[22]

This trend began to reverse itself following the Napoleonic con-
cordat (1801), and especially following the Charter of 1814, according to which Catholicism became the religion of state. Having
been placed by Napoleon in a state of "liberté surveillée," the
Church benefited more than a little under the Restoration from
an anti-Revolutionary sentiment and what can only be described
as a new era of closer relations between "altar and throne." This
is not to imply that the robe recovered anything like the power it
had enjoyed under the Ancien Régime. On the contrary, the
Church of the middle decades of the nineteenth century remained
deeply divided between Gallicans and Ultramontanes. Furthermore, it was still weakened by the disappearance of educational
centers and by a relative lack of numbers, and it remained irreme-
diably aggravated by the Voltarian spirit of a fundamentally anti-
clerical bourgeoisie. Religious history was not taught except at the
Sorbonne. Theological faculties were still practically nonexistent
except for Paris, where teaching was for the most part secular;
this in contrast to the contemporaneous explosion of other fields
in the post-Napoleonic era—literature, art history, oriental studies, paleontology, the political and social sciences. And, perhaps
most important of all, the Guizot law of 1833, which provided for
government support and regulation of public schools, removed
the whole area of primary and secondary education from Church
jurisdiction, leading, in David Pinkney's phrase, to "France's last
religious war."[23]

The spirit of the Restoration, combined with the Romantic return to Christianity (and to the Middle Ages), which was less
theological than sentimental and esthetic, produced "a Catholic

Renewal" or "Restoration"—a second ecclesiastical wind in the struggle against what must have been perceived as an irreversible progressive encroachment of the secular state. Here one thinks not only of members of the clergy like Doms Guéranger and Pitra, who revived the Benedictine priory at Solesmes and who were also directly involved in the patrologies, but of the revival of the Dominican, Carthusian, and Trappist orders, and of Emmanuel d'Alzon's establishment of the Assumptionist Fathers in order to overturn the secularism of the Revolution. One thinks of Catholic intellectuals such as Lamennais, whose *Essai sur l'indifférence en matière de religion* (1817) renewed Christian apologetics; the abbé Genoude, whose sixteen-volume translation of the Bible and twelve-volume *Raison du christianisme* enjoyed enormous success; the royalist and papist Joseph de Maistre; Louis de Bonald; Jean-Baptiste Lacordaire; Félix Dupanloup; the theologian Gerbert; the polemicist Charles de Montalembert, who proposed in his pamphlet *Du Devoir des catholiques dans la question de la liberté de l'enseignement* (1843) the formation of a Catholic party to fight for "free" schools; the poet and Christian apologist Chateaubriand, whose *Génie du christianisme* (1802) constituted in some profound sense the birth certificate of these new fathers of the Church. One thinks too of the quixotic and often highly polemic religious newspapers in whose development, as we shall see, Migne played such a large role—Picot's *l'Ami de la religion,* Michaud's *La Quotidienne,* and, a little later, Lamennais's *l'Avenir.*

The Church recuperated during the Restoration (1815–30) some of the strength in numbers which it had lost after 1789. To the 36,000 priests in 1814, of which 42 percent were older than sixty, we find in 1830 40,600 priests, of which 29 percent were older than sixty, and in 1848 47,000 priests, of which only 5.6 percent were over sixty. Thus there was a steady growth in numbers of an increasingly younger clergy during the reigns of both Louis XVIII and Charles X as well as during the July Monarchy (1830–48) of Louis-Philippe. Seminaries increased from 103 to 224 during the Restoration, and the number of ordinations doubled from 1,185 in 1816 to 2,357 in 1830. Female clergy grew from 12,343 in 1808 to some 31,000 in 1831.[24]

It is in this spirit of religious restoration—a Catholic Enlightenment—that one can best situate Migne, whose unique contribution was the reparation of what he saw as a lack of libraries and of texts. Indeed, from the beginning Migne makes the connection between the *Bibliothèque universelle du clergé* and the uncertainty of the times. "The commentators and theologians of ancient times . . . lived in relative calm, and nothing troubled their solitude. . . . They lived in profound security, sheltered from harsh laws which protected them; and we, the children of revolutions, live always afraid, like the bird on a tree planted in the middle of the public square" (AN F18 1803). Migne links, moreover, the fate of the Ateliers catholiques to that of Catholicism itself. "In a word," he writes in the attempt to guarantee the scholarly quality of the volumes, "if these *Cours* were not good, then Catholicism itself would be impotent to produce anything even remotely comparable; for there can be nothing better than the masterpieces produced by its living organs!" The eventual victory of Catholicism is inextricably associated with Migne's editorial success: "Catholicism will certainly have brought off a great victory the day when the world and the clergy will be convinced that there exists at last a *Cours d'Ecriture Sainte et de Théologie*" (AN F18 1803).

Like so many instances of Migne's own writing, the above, aimed at selling books, can be taken to be supremely self-serving. There is an undeniably egotistical—even childish—element in the implication that if the *Cours* are not good then nothing can be good, that if they do not succeed then religion cannot succeed. Yet, of this there can be little doubt: Migne saw his own mission as that of saving the "patrimony of the Church."[25] And to save it in a special way. The *Bibliothèque universelle du clergé* was founded on social, esthetic, and economic principles whose synthesis embodies a seeming unawareness of contradiction and a refusal to compromise characteristic of all that Migne did. Thus, the first of Migne's principles was that of broad access—"We will have as ours the consolation of having rendered the *Patrologie* **accessible** and **intelligible** to all"[26]—which implies the second, that of moderate cost: "My fixed goal is to popularize among the clergy the masterpieces of Catholicism through low prices and an elegant presentation" (see below, pp. 79–84).[27]

Toward that end Migne associated himself with the most pow-

erful clerical figures of the "reconstruction catholique," Dom Guéranger and Dom Pitra. Guéranger, who in fact first suggested the
project of the patrologies, was an early collaborator and signed a
contract with Migne such that Benedictines of Solesmes would
edit the *Cours* and would have sole responsibility for its doctrinal contents, typography, and tables.[28] The collaboration with
Solesmes, calling for three volumes per month, was abandoned,
however, when Guéranger failed to obtain the consent of his
monks, suspicious of the very tenacity of Migne's character that
would have made such a project possible in the first place. Should
they fall behind in the schedule agreed upon, they feared they
would not only lose financially, but he might pursue them legally.
"One of the fears on which they dwelled the most," Dom
Gardereau wrote to Dom Guéranger on April 20, 1842, "is that in
case of significant delay, not only would the honoraria be lost, but
Migne would sue us for damages with interest."[29] It was clear
from the start that Dom Guéranger was no match for the financial
wizardry of Migne. Indeed, as Guéranger's sister Cécile Bruyère,
first abbess of Saint-Cécile de Solesmes, insists, "Dom Guéranger
has never managed to understand the raw reality of a figure."[30]
The break with Solesmes did not, however, put an end to the
collaboration between Migne and Dom Guéranger, who continued
to collect the books necessary for the patrologies. Then too, it was
Guéranger who recommended to Migne Dom Pitra, who was not
afraid of signing a contract with Migne in 1843, thus assuming
the role of "chief architect" of the project of the *Cours complets*.

The monks of Solesmes were no match for Migne, whose ambition and capacity for work place him among the epic entrepreneurial figures of the century. Indeed, this "Rastignac auvergnat en
soutane" (Pierre Pierrard) is often compared to that other printing
giant in whose *Comédie humaine* he could so easily have figured
(more later).[31] The Ateliers catholiques represented, as contemporary witnesses confirm, an enormous undertaking. At any given
time Migne employed hundreds of workers—typesetters, smelters,
manuscript and copy editors, printers, proofreaders, binders, cou-
riers, and accountants. The approximately 300 employees of 1842
had almost doubled by 1854 (to 596), and Migne claimed that he
had an equal number working on the outside.[32] This was, by any

reckoning, an enormous industrial plant. As Frédéric Barbier has shown, for example, a survey of the printing industry of 77 departments (Paris *intra muros* and Rhône excluded) in 1851 reveals 6,657 workers for 627 print shops or roughly 11 workers, including foremen, per operation. Balzac in the late 1820s employed only 36; the firm of Firmin Didot, 200.[33] Nor was the printing industry an exception. The 125,000 largest French manufacturers of the Restoration employed on an average only 10 workers each. Few great industrialists of the period could claim as many workers as the Ateliers catholiques: The Cunin-Gridaine sheet factory employed 500 workers for an annual production of over five million francs; Nicolas Schlumberger had 700 in his metallurgical works. Both were considered to be major enterprises.[34]

An Industrial City of God

TO JUDGE BY the final product—the more than a thousand books that constitute the *Bibliothèque universelle du clergé*—it is clear that the Ateliers catholiques represented, above all, a book factory—"a Catholic industrial palace" ("un palais à l'industrie catholique"), according to Hippolyte Barbier, whose account of a visit to "le Petit Montrouge, près des barrières d'Enfer et du Maine" (presently number 189, at the corner of the rue Thibaud) depicts as early as 1841 Migne the industrialist filling orders from around the world, circulating among his workers: "The master visits his hundred and forty typesetters and printers; he perhaps revises the proofs of St. Augustine or St. Chrysostom, etc. He takes care of his vast correspondence with the bishops around the world." The visitor was most impressed, however, by the enormous effects of mechanical energy—the clouds of steam, the heat of the foundry furnace—emanating from Migne's book machine:

. . . go there, he will extend a hand; and you will see functioning through the power of steam the five great mechanical presses which he just set up in the back of the building; you will cross this immense workshop filled, like billowing black clouds, with sheets laid out for drying. Here the foundry men who mold typeface before a furnace; there tables set for folding; there again the men of his accounting services, and from the proofreaders' office.[35]

Migne was fascinated by the efficiency of the mechanical press and sings its praises in one of his printed advertisement broadsheets: "Steam is harnessed to mechanical power, and their force of production is such that they can give birth to 2,000 volumes in quarto every 24 hours" (AN F18, 369).

And well Migne might have been proud: the application of steam power to printing was, even at mid-century, still relatively rare. Figures from the year 1861, that is, six years after the *Patrologia Latina* had been completed and five years before the completion of the *Patrologia Graeca,* show that the 74 *départements* of France, covering 684 print shops, possessed a total of 117 steam-driven presses. Forty-four *départements* (or 60 percent of the total) possessed no steam-driven press at all. This means that one in three of the 364 printers located in the remaining 30 *départements* worked to some degree by steam. Fifty-seven machines were to be found in "La Seine." Thus, when Migne brags about the productive resources of the Ateliers catholiques, he lays claim to approximately 10 percent of the steam-driven printing capacity of an entire highly mechanized *département.*[36] Nor was such capability merely quantitative: the efficiency of the mechanical steam press allowed a concentration of labor, a compression of time whose economy of scale affected the price of the patrologies and lay, as we shall see, at the heart of Migne's industrio-spiritual project.

Migne created much more than a simple print shop. He fashioned an autonomous universe dedicated to the book. The Ateliers catholiques contained a library, a bookstore, a chapel, a bindery, a foundry, a warehouse, an artist's atelier, and Migne's own apartment, in addition to the workshops and the factory in which the *Bibliothèque universelle du clergé* was actually printed. Migne conceived the Ateliers catholiques along the lines of ancient models— the cathedral building site, but also the medieval scriptorium, against which he measured his own productive capacity; one minute of the industrial present was worth three years of another age. "Then too, the hand of a monk of yesteryear could not copy in three years what is done in the Imprimerie catholique in a single minute."[37] Most of all, Migne envisioned the company he had founded in terms of the monastery and the cloister, whose communal perfection he recreated in the banlieu of Paris.[38] The Ateliers catholiques were a miniature City of God. "The first time I visited the abbé Migne at Montrouge," writes R. du Merzer in the popular magazine *L'Illustration,* "an employee said to me: come into the warehouse, take Bible Street on your right, then Bossuet Street on your left, and at the end you will find M. l'abbé Migne on Fathers of the Church Square. I crossed long aisles formed of enormous piles of books in quarto and at the far end I found the abbé Migne pointing out, on Fathers of the Church Square, the place reserved for Tertullian's building."[39]

Migne Brewer of Catholic Books

MIGNE'S RELATION TO the monastery, not to mention the City of God, was, however, at best ambiguous. Committed by the very nature of the *Bibliothèque universelle du clergé* to appear to maintain a certain distance from the material world, he was nonetheless obliged to operate powerfully within it. He uses, in fact, the model of the medieval corpus of monks, at once withdrawn from the secular world and contributing intellectually to it, to legitimate the matter of his publications—"But that which accounts for their superiority, that which rendered them learned and eloquent, was the fact that, where they were concerned, prayer was the great foundation of study"—and he uses it to justify his own worldliness, even his will toward domination: "Moreover, the men of whom we speak were the living glory of their *society;* motivated by a powerful 'esprit de *corps,*' they spared no effort in order that their spirit might conquer all others" (AN F18 1803).

The reality of the workplace was far from ideal. Migne was a formidable taskmaster, and the Ateliers catholiques resembled more a feudal manor, of which he was the lord, than the ideal city rendered by the names of its streets. Migne himself showed little charity in dealing with the outside world. And there is no more powerful illustration of this than the contract he negotiated for the actual *City of God.* A letter of October 14, 1841, to an editor whom he called Dupner (later "Dubner," and whose real name was Dübner) shows just how hard a bargain the entrepreneurial abbé could drive. Migne presses him for delivery of the *City of God* "before Thursday, or Friday at the latest": "Monsieur," he writes, "I have the misfortune to inform you that 60 typesetters will be out of work if you do not come to their aid with the *City of God* of St. Augustine on Thursday, or Friday at the latest" (BN n. a. 6143, fol. 240). Should Dübner refuse, Migne is prepared simply to reprint the edition of the Benedictines (see below, p. 59). And, as we have seen, Migne's tenacity where subscribers to the *Bibliothèque universelle* were concerned pushed him to pursue a debtor "even to California."

Within the walls of the Ateliers catholiques Migne appears to have exploited his editors and workers in the mold of any nineteenth-century capitalist entrepreneur. Leaving aside for the moment the relations of Migne and his chief editor, Dom Pitra, whose name was practically erased from the patrologies, there can be no doubt that Migne paid his workers badly, which is not without its hidden blessing for the historian. Because he paid them badly, they were often discontent; because they were discontent, they came to the attention of the authorities; and because they came to the attention of the authorities, we are able to recover to some extent their story. "Last September 29th," we read in a letter from the Cabinet du Préfet de Police to the Ministre de l'Instruction Publique et des Cultes written on October 27, 1857,

you informed me that the workers of the print shop of M. l'abbé Migne at Montrouge were brought to your attention for showing a very bad political spirit, and you asked me to inquire as to whether the head of this establishment was at all responsible for such tendencies. Three hundred and fifty to four hundred workers on the average, women included, work in the ateliers of the abbé Migne. As the salaries he offers are low, he accepts just about any worker who shows up without worrying too much about their past; usually they don't stay long in his workshops and leave as soon as they find something better elsewhere. (AN F19 5842)[40]

Not only badly paid, the workers of the Ateliers catholiques also submitted to conditions which even the police inspector found harsh. Migne imposed a regime of silence according to which the medieval monachal rule became indistinguishable from that of the factory worker of the industrial revolution. "He enforces, furthermore, in his print shop a severe discipline which he has rigorously observed; thus it is expressly forbidden to sing or to engage in even the most frivolous conversation while working" (AN F19 5842).

The silence imposed upon Migne's workers did not prevent disputes with them. On the contrary, the Ministre de l'Intérieur (Direction de la Presse) characterizes him in a report of December 23, 1853, later repeated in a report of Inspector Gaillard of February 1854, as "a violent man who often has rows with his employees" ("un homme violent qui a souvent des rixes avec ses employés") (AN F18 283 and F18 333a). He is perceived by the authorities as an unstable character, a source of constant trouble. "[Migne] is known for his troublesome, pesky, confused spirit," the Ministre de l'Intérieur notes on May 3, 1854. "One must watch out for constant abuse on his part" (AN F18 333a).

And constant abuses there were. As Pierre Pierrard notes, Migne seems to have quarreled with just about everyone: with, as we have seen, Mgr de Beauregard; and later with Mgr Affre, Archbishop of Paris; with Dom Pitra; with the booksellers (libraires) of Paris; with the editors of l'Univers; with his collaborators Prompsault and Picot (the director of l'Ami de la religion); with his brother; with Jules Gordon of La Voix de la vérité; with the entire editorial board of the Journal des faits; and, finally, with a M. Gasnier, Papetier, with whom Migne had dealings over the ownership of the Journal des faits that came practically to physical blows. "L'abbé Migne only began paying after having received notice from a notary," the Ministre de l'Intérieur (Direction de la Sûreté Générale) notes on December 21, 1853. "He had a discussion with a Sr. Gasnier, a paper supplier and creditor of the Journal des faits, in the course of which gross insults were publicly exchanged and which practically ended in blows."[41] Eugène Veuillot reports that his brother Louis Veuillot, editor of L'Univers from 1843 on, characterized Migne not only as "having an abrupt manner and way of speaking," but as being capable of fits of rage and even violence at the slightest provocation. To wit: as Migne left the newspaper offices one evening toward midnight in the company of one of the early editors, Melchior du Lac, the two were harassed by two pedestrians who cried "Couac! couac!" "Immediately the abbé Migne, as stocky as he was and armed with his umbrella, lunged at them and struck them, crying: 'Scoundrels! I'll show you of what stuff a priest is made!'"[42] The incident recalls, of course, Migne's act of resistance to the secular authorities in the early days of the July Monarchy (above, p. 6) and, again, offers some clue as to what it must have been like to work for the temperamental and tenacious abbé.

If the suspicious Préfet watched the industrious priest, it was not because the low wages of the Ateliers catholiques called for the enforcement of fair labor laws, but because low wages necessarily meant a restless, unstable population. The police note that Migne's workers find positions elsewhere as soon as possible, and this renders the task of surveillance more difficult.[43] But the Ateliers catholiques represented more than just a mobile work force, for Migne deliberately recruited workers from the most dispossessed element of the population, not only unstable, but vulnerable by definition to his offers of low wages. "He welcomes at Montrouge all the suspect characters who cannot find work in Paris," the police inspector writes (AN F18 333a). Migne actively recruited workers with announcements in his prospectuses or, as in the present example, on the letterhead of his stationery, and the initial invitation seems innocent enough: "We only print for ourselves, but if a brother seeks as a refuge the shelter of our presses, we know how to be of service" (BN n. a. 6138 fol. 38). Hippolyte Barbier too makes the Ateliers catholiques seem like a philanthropic organization, the equivalent of the present-day Salvation Army or homeless shelter where destitute souls might be redeemed by hard work: "Any priest, no matter who he is, and who is hungry and seeks employment, can knock on the door of the Imprimerie catholique. He must only promise to live as he should live; and if he does so, he will be saved."[44]

Yet, reality, again, differed from the rhetoric of both prospectus and biography. The demimonde of the Ateliers catholiques attracted, as in a Balzacian tale, political "refugees" of the Revolution as well as of the revolutions of 1830 and 1848. More important, the safe house of Montrouge welcomed priests who, like Migne himself, had had trouble with the ecclesiastical hierarchy. This fact must have been generally known and does not escape the frères Goncourt, who poke merciless fun at Migne observing the police observing him: "A curious character of a priest, this abbé

Migne, a brewer of Catholic books. He has set up in Vaugirard a print shop full of proscribed priests, like him, of defrocked rogues (*sacripants défroqués*), of death cheaters (*des Trompe-la-Mort*) who have been cast out of grace, and who, upon the very sight of a police inspector, jump for the doors. . . . There emerges out of there editions of the Fathers, encyclopedias in 500 volumes."[45] At the highest level of his administration, Migne surrounded himself with abbés who opposed their bishop—l'abbé Prompsault, l'abbé Clavel, l'abbé Raymond, l'abbé André, and the defrocked occultist Alphonse Constant (Eliphas Lévy).[46] But even within the ranks, the Ateliers catholiques represented a haven for those who were "in bad odor" with the Church or were married, some with dependents.[47] "L'abbé Migne is unfavorably represented in the reports of his conduct and morality," reads a report from the Cabinet du Préfet de Police of January 31, 1854. "He is known as a schemer (*intrigant*) and surrounds himself with all the priests on the index throughout the dioceses of France" (AN F18, 333a).

If Migne welcomed defrocked priests from all dioceses of France, he had a special predilection for those who came from his native Auvergne. "No one is unaware," reads an article in *La Haute-Auvergne* of 1857, "of the cordial hospitality that workers find chez M. Migne, especially those who come from Saint-Flour; he is for them a father more than a master, and his goodness helps them to find, far from home, all the sweetness of family life."[48] Once there, however, the numerous apprentices and workers found the wages insufficient. The chanoine Virbonnet intervened, requesting, for example, that "this young man whose family is poor should be received by you under better conditions than you impose upon him." The son Ajalbert of Saint-Flour complained to his father "that he is unable still to earn a livelihood." Migne's response, on the other hand, is almost comic: the Auvergnats of today are not worth those of yesteryear, he maintains; and those who leave Auvergne are, in the theme so dear to the nineteenth century, corrupted by Paris.[49] As indeed Migne might have been corrupted by the demographics of the 1840s. The increase in population of rural France created in this period a surplus of labor, pushed, by the lack of agricultural employment, toward industrialized cities.[50] Following the centripetal movement toward Paris, the

Auvergnat and other workers of the Ateliers catholiques belonged to a work force that must have been not only mobile, but, because of its very transitory nature, also vulnerable to the rapacious abbé's blessed exploitation.

The police surveillance of the Ateliers catholiques focused primarily upon Migne himself, who is suspected repeatedly of a disloyalty to the regime that can, in any case, never be proven. "He is believed to lean in the direction of the Legitimists; but he knows how to adapt his behavior to the situation," writes the Préfet to the Ministre de l'Intérieur in 1854. "He voted in 1848 for General Cavaignac, today he proclaims his devotion to the Emperor; and, in short, he is a man in whom one can have no confidence" (AN F18 333a). The same inspector who notes (October 27, 1865) that the low wages of the Ateliers catholiques necessarily imply a mobile work force concludes that, given the large number of workers, some no doubt have a "bad attitude," but that the majority "appear healthy and favorable to the government of the Emperor." He reports that when a subscription was taken up at the time of the birth of the Prince Impérial, 360 workers of the Ateliers catholiques were on the list and that Migne sent the money on to M. le Commissaire de Police of the commune. "The sympathies of M. l'abbé Migne for the government of the Emperor are perhaps not very strong," he concludes, "but he has never shown ill will: preoccupied above all with the interests of his business, he would be the first, we think, to repress any hostile activity that might break out in his print shop" (AN F19 5842).

Migne's own entrepreneurial spirit, not to mention his financial investment, would seem to have discouraged anything resembling a progressive social attitude. On the contrary, in a deposition of August 13, 1853, to the Directeur de la Sûreté Générale, Migne, who was involved at the time in a lengthy quarrel over the ownership of the *Journal des faits,* affirms his faith in "property rights, that is to say, the most sacred thing in the world after religion" (AN F18 369). And in a broadsheet printed in three columns and sent on November 11, 1853, to the stockholders of the same *Journal des faits,* he evokes with horror the image of apocalyptic social upheaval in a rhetorical flourish intended to win them to his side against his opponent M. Vassal: "*To sum everything up,* the employee revolts against his boss, the proxy against the founder, the foreigner against the rightful heir, the pretender against the owner, the one under whom everything has perished against the one who can restore it all; finally, the one who is nothing against the one who should be all" (AN F18 369).

Plagiarism and the Press

Migne Journaliste

IN ONE OF the prospectuses printed for the purpose of selling the *Cours complets,* Migne contrasts the thoughtful long study of the Fathers with what he perceives to be the narrow journalism of the present day. "What would a journalist say," he asks, "accustomed as he is to exaggerate everything, if, instead of seeing arrive in his offices a young man all radiant with self-satisfaction, because he holds in his hands a brochure containing a few half-blank pages, he would see before him an old monk holding a few of these enormous volumes full of knowledge, and to which monks were not afraid of devoting 40 or 50 years of their life?" (AN F18 1803).

The question is worth asking, but it takes on special meaning given the fact that Migne himself owned and edited at least ten newspapers in the course of his lifetime. At once a "brewer of Catholic books" and a journalist, he led a double existence as someone who, to repeat the Préfet's phrase, "knows how to adapt his behavior to the situation." Moreover, if he was watched by the police, it was not only because the work force of the Ateliers catholiques represented an element of potential social unrest, but because Migne's other publications made the publicist a significant shaper of public, and especially clerical, opinion during the July Monarchy, the Second Republic, and the Second Empire.

Migne's double life of publicist and patrologist has, again, a common origin in the suppression of *On Freedom, by a Priest,* which led him to leave Puiseaux under the episcopal constraint from which emanated an inexhaustible urge to write. The *exeat* signed by the Bishop of Orléans in fact makes no mention of the patrologies for which he is remembered and which almost certainly had not yet entered his consciousness, but specifies instead that "M. Jacques-Paul Migne, former curé of the parish of the canton of Puiseaux . . . is of sound moral character. . . . He has distinguished himself by his faith, his piety, his zeal, his love of work. . . . He has conducted himself with prudence and energy under difficult circumstances, and he only leaves the diocese, much to our regret, in order to devote himself to a newspaper called the *Univers religieux,* by which he hopes to do good works."[1] Migne, who had in just about all he did an uncanny instinct for the market, on the one hand sensed an opportunity opened by the disappearance of Lamennais's financially ailing *l'Avenir* in 1831, and on the other hand feared that the religious press would shift to the side of the Gallicans and Legitimists through the dominance of Picot's *l'Ami de la religion.*[2] Once again, it is impossible to tell whether the abbé's motivations were profoundly self-interested or altruistic, whether he was drawn to the capital by the love of capital or, as the Bishop maintains, because "he hopes to do good works." In either case, Migne's departure from Puiseaux is the classic nineteenth-century success story of a provincial in Paris, though it is hard to equate his trajectory from rags to riches with anything resembling either social ascension or economic ambition, since, for the abstemious abbé, who lived more like a miser than a bourgeois, the social hardly counted at all; and his fortune was, as we shall see, hardly personal.

Installed in Paris on the rue des Fossés-Saint-Jacques, Migne sent prospectuses to all the bishops of France announcing the forthcoming publication of two newspapers, *l'Univers religieux* and *Le Spectateur,* the latter being merely a screen, a "straw newspaper," and the first of Migne's journalistic publicity stunts or double newspaper ventures, since *Le Spectateur* disappeared as soon as *l'Univers religieux* was established.[3] In the announcement for *l'Univers religieux* can be seen in germ many of the traits of style as well as the essential elements characteristic of the *Bibliothèque universelle du clergé.* And it may in fact have been in the early days of *l'Univers religieux,* that is in late 1833, that Migne first conceived of the project of editing the Church Fathers. One of the earliest articles signed Jean d'Aure, a pseudonym for Melchior du Lac, an early editorial associate who would become editor of *l'Univers religieux* between the time of Migne's departure in 1836 and Louis Veuillot's arrival in the early 1840s, is entitled *Lettres familières sur les Pères de l'Eglise—Première lettre: Des connaissances les plus utiles à l'étude des Saints Pères.* As in the patrologies that would be *"accessible* and **intelligible** to all," Migne proposes to address in *l'Univers religieux* the widest possible public—"to all manner of people living in the world, to thinking youth and to men of good faith and of all opinions, as well as to members of the French and foreign Catholic clergy." Filling an important pedagogical gap, *l'Univers religieux* will be for members of the clergy "a reminder of what is taught in [religious] courses and a supplement to what is not taught." It will, in consonance with Migne's own totalizing disposition, be encyclopedic: "The editors are so to speak on the track of all that is done or is published in books or newspapers or by learned societies for and against Catholicism." Because it unites an encyclopedic amount of material in a limited space it shows the tendency, also evident elsewhere, toward compression—the condensation of intellectual effort associated, again, with the mechanical efficiency of the steam engine. *l'Univers religieux* will treat all subjects, mixing theological considerations with more practical matters of daily life: "We will present the most Catholic interpretations of the questions that are the most interesting according to their relevance to the present— dances, theatrical balls, novels, interest-bearing loans, various taxes, divorce, the salaries of clergy, of priests . . . the whole with the greatest discretion." Finally, in the spirit of the anonymity characteristic of Migne's other journalistic ventures as well as of the patrologies, *l'Univers religieux* will be completely neutral, its sources displaced upon the discourse of others in such a way as to render absent Migne's own editorial voice. Forbidding "almost all discussions," *l'Univers religieux* will report only "facts, laws, decrees, debates in the chambers and the editorial opinion of newspapers on every major event."[4] The epigraph of *l'Univers religieux*—and here one must bear in mind the importance for Migne of epigraphs alongside of the letterheads on his stationery—was "Unity in matters that are certain, freedom in doubtful ones, charity, truth, objectivity in all" ("Unité dans les choses certaines, liberté dans les douteuses, charité, verité, impartialité dans toutes"), phrases that from the beginning capture, in a summary, practically telegraphic style, the spirit of all of Migne's publishing ventures, including the patrologies, throughout his journalistic and editorial career.

Migne could not have been luckier. With the prospectus dispatched in September 1833, he had by October, and even before the appearance of the first number, not only made *Le Spectateur* disappear, but also acquired a second newspaper, whose editor, the timid and unworldly Emmanuel Bailly, proposed that the *l'Univers religieux* absorb *La Tribune catholique,* which was itself an obscure avatar of *l'Avenir.* The first volume of *l'Univers religieux,* printed on the Presses de Bailly, 2 Place de la Sorbonne, appeared on November 3, 1833, and after that every day but Monday until Migne changed the name the following year to *l'Univers*—and until the entrepreneurial abbé encountered the first in a long series of legal battles involving almost every aspect of his journalistic activity. On October 23, 1834, less than a year after the first appearance of *l'Univers religieux,* Picot, editor of the rival *Ami de la religion,* in a passage worth citing at length, accused Migne of plagiarism:

L'Univers copies everything, ecclesiastical news and political reflections. . . . Its editors were at a loss to find sufficient material, so they were obliged to go fishing in various collections of articles which do not fit in at all with the plans of a religious newspaper, while at present they have found an already worked mine which furnishes abundant material. . . . This useful idea and a convenient tactic encourages laziness. L'Univers is short three or four columns to fill a particular volume: quick, a pair of scissors; in two minutes, it will have solved its little problem. . . . Such a fine discovery deserves to be cited in the annals of plagiarism.[5]

On December 24, 1835, Migne was convicted by the Tribunal de Police Correctionnelle de la Seine of attempting to bribe a postal employee and sentenced to pay a fine of two hundred francs.[6] He left *l'Univers* in 1836.

The Truth and the Facts

BY 1838 MIGNE had installed himself in Montrouge and founded, one can assume with the five thousand francs obtained from sale of his shares of *l'Univers* to Bailly, the Ateliers catholiques. A document signed by the Ministre de l'Intérieur on February 15, 1839, accords a "bookseller's license" (*brevet de libraire*) to Victor Migne, his brother, who is also granted by the mayor and the town council of the commune of Montrouge permission to install a print shop. Jacques-Paul Migne does not, however, reenter the world of journalism until 1846, with the founding of the newspaper whose very name is the voice of truth, *La Voix de la vérité*, which appeared in both a daily and a triweekly edition until it was divided (1854) into a daily called simply *La Vérité* and a biweekly which kept the original name.[7] This amounted to a stock split, since Migne's chief motive seems to have been the sale of two *Vérités* where there had once been only one. Nor was the procedure, worthy, again, of a place in Balzac's *Comédie humaine*, unknown to the novelist: the character Finot, whose very name is a homonym—"finaud"—for the finesse of the financial maneuver, proposes something similar to the chief protagonist of the *Illusions perdues*, Lucien de Rubempré, who will serve, like Migne's brother or another substitute, as a "borrowed name" for a newspaper operation in which Lucien's mistress's benefactor Matifat will supply the money:

"My dear fellow," Finot then said to Etienne. "I have Dauriat's word. I'm in for a third share in the ownership of the weekly paper. I've settled for thirty thousand francs cash down on condition that I become editor and director. . . . I clinched the bargain without having more than ten thousand francs of my own. Listen. If you can get Matifat to buy the half of my share—one-sixth—I'll make you editor of my little newspaper with a salary of two hundred and fifty francs a month. You will be my figurehead [*prête-nom*]. I want to maintain control of the editing and keep all my interests in it while appearing to have no hand in it."[8]

Migne sold *La Vérité* in 1856 to Jules Bordot, who sold it in turn, before it became the *Courrier de Paris* and then disappeared completely in 1859. After several attempts to dispose of *La Voix de la vérité*, Migne finally sold it to Eugène Taconet, who was authorized on February 17, 1860, to change its name to *Le Monde*, having merged it with the surviving version of Migne's original *l'Univers*.[9]

Even before he had sold the double *Vérité*, Migne founded on May 31, 1850, another newspaper, one aimed more toward a secular than a clerical readership—the *Journal des faits*. Victor Migne again held the "brevet," though the actual manager was a Guillaume Vassal, who just two months later, not content to be the vassal of an ecclesiastical lord, formed a separate corporation with Victor, the articles of constitution of which excluded Migne altogether. Migne sued Vassal and his brother in the Tribunal de Commerce before the matter was settled out of court at the behest of the Migne family.[10] Yet the dispute over the ownership and the direction of the *Journal des faits* lasted for over three years.[11] When Victor Migne died unexpectedly in July 1853, Vassal named as editor a certain Frédéric Delbrel, whom Migne rejected, accusing both Delbrel and Vassal of disinheriting his brother's children. The *Journal des faits* was put up for auction as a result of all the squabbling over ownership and finally became Migne's on December 20, 1853, for the sum of forty-one thousand francs. It was, however, closed down by the government on February 10, 1854, as a result of two condemnations, one for printing false news and the other for fraudulent copying (*contrefaçon*) of articles from *Le Constitutionnel*.

Seen from a wider perspective, such accusations merely served as excuses to repress a printing operation that was, as we shall see, simultaneously censured by the Archbishop of Paris and considered to be potentially unfriendly to the regime.[12] Such pressure was, further, in keeping with the general trend just during the Second Republic and Empire, and after a period of relative freedom during the Restoration, toward increased surveillance and control of the press and, more generally, of the printing industry.[13] A law of July 27, 1849, submitted to the appropriate authority all book distribution. The coup d'état of December 1851, which reinstated the necessity of a government stamp before a book could appear, also instituted a decree according to which newspapers were brought under a regime of surveillance and could be warned, suspended, or eliminated by simple administrative decision. A commission was established in 1854 for the purpose of examining all books submitted for the required official authorization.[14]

An internal memorandum of the Ministère de l'Intérieur, Direction de la Sûreté Générale, no date, takes cognizance of the fact that "M. l'abbé Migne finds himself thus in the special situation of having bought or having paid for a newspaper which will disappear at the very moment he is in a position to take possession of it, without this disappearance having been caused by his action." Migne's request for an exception to the law against operating more than one newspaper at a time meets with the Minister's disapproval on the grounds that such an exception would weaken the government's control over the press.[15] Migne, moreover, suspected of legitimist leanings, was not judged by the authorities of the Empire to merit such an exception: "According to the information obtained in his case, [l'abbé Migne] does not appear worthy of this extraordinary favor, and the incident which puts the *Journal des faits* under the order of suppression should not have happened since he would no doubt never have obtained under *his own name* the authorization which he requests. To sum up his situation, he is a man 'with a bad reputation because of his conduct and his morality' [*mal représenté pour la conduite et la moralité*]; having had several judgments against him, offering no political guarantees, his status as a censured priest [*son caractère de prêtre (censuré)*] only adds to the difficulties of his situation" (AN F18 333a).

The twisted fate of the *Journal des faits* captures much of Migne's journalistic career, which takes the appearance of an accretion of fictions. Thus, he had at the outset placed the "license" in his brother's name, with Victor Migne and Vassal serving as the front men for his actual operation of the newspaper. When, however, Victor died and Vassal attempted to seize the capital of the corporation, Migne was forced to admit the original ruse. And in a rhetorical flourish worthy of the early Christian apologists, he argues against granting the *Journal des faits* to the man who had functioned until then as his legal cover, his "strawman manager"(*gérant de paille*), to invoke the phrase which Migne repeats more than once.[16] For the Directeur de la Sûreté Générale to rule in favor of Vassal would mean, Migne maintains, to rule against the family and society.[17] It would be to deny the "sacred right" of succession and to "turn upside down" the legal code.[18] It would, finally, be an act of "socialistic" disappropriation that menaced the very concept of private property, which, for Migne, as we have seen, is sacred: "You will see necessarily that in maintaining M. Vassal as part of the administration of a newspaper where he merely serves as a simple and bad employee would be to sacrifice for a legal fiction the legal authority which has named me, and it would be to sacrifice property rights, that is to say, the most sacred thing in the world after religion."[19]

Pressed by the Ministre de l'Intérieur for the true names of those legally responsible for the *Journal des faits,* Migne, in a response also worthy of the great Jesuitical thinkers, denies the need for an editor of a "feuille de simple reproduction":

In response to your letter of yesterday, December 15, which asks me to provide without delay the necessary authorization—required by the first article of the statute of February 17, 1852—as owner and for the editors: as director, co-managing editor, and administrator of the *Journal des faits,* I have the honor of asking you to note that this newspaper, being a simple reprint digest, does not need an editor-in-chief; that, being produced in my *print shops* along with my other publications and another newspaper, nothing is easier for me than both to administer and to direct it myself; in the final analysis, I have no intention of taking a co-managing editor.

If, however, Migne's request to be recognized "simultaneously as owner, managing editor, administrator, and director of the *Journal des faits* as I am of the *Voix de la vérité*" should prove to be unacceptable, he proposes yet another substitute—"and if, in your wisdom, you find something which prevents your investing in me this double managerial role, I then propose as managing editor M. Pierre Blot de Poly, from Yonne."[20]

The offer seems honest enough. Except, as it turns out, Pierre Blot de Poly is no less of a strawman, and the legal fiction is doubled by a specious social promotion. According to the police report and two internal memoranda of the Ministère de l'Intérieur, Direction de la Sûreté Générale, Migne has fabricated for M. Blot a "title of nobility" (*titre de noblesse*). A confidential letter of December 21, 1853, informs the Minister of Migne's having become adjudicataire of the *Journal des faits* for forty-one thousand francs, of his row with Gasnier, of the battle with Vassal and Delbrel over ownership of the paper, and of Migne's political opportunism.

He is believed to lean in the direction of the Legitimists; but he knows how to adapt his behavior to the situation. . . . As for M. Blot, whom he has presented as managing editor and whom he has taken the trouble to name Blot de Poly in order to give him a patina of nobility intended to fool the Legitimist party, the man is a worker, a typesetter, in his print shop and his real name is Pierre Blot, born in Poly (Yonne).[21]

Nor can there be any doubt concerning Migne's motives, which are the same as those which governed his earlier use of brother

Victor. It is illegal to own and operate more than one newspaper at a time, and thus both the real brother and false noble serve as legal fictions behind which Migne maintains control of the truth and the facts, *La Voix de la vérité* and *Le Journal des faits.*[22]

Here we touch upon one of the myriad of ambiguities that seem to emanate from Migne's person as well as from the enterprise of the Ateliers catholiques. That is, on the surface, and in the context of the historian's tendency to assign interested intention to individual agency, it looks as though Migne's use of Victor and Vassal as strawmen, the one a false owner and the other a false manager (*gérant*), to make it appear he operates only one newspaper at a time is nothing more than an attempt to protect his own investment. One could suppose that for the clever abbé, brotherly love was especially a matter of the "sacredness" of private property. But the use of others is so entirely of a piece with the editorial modus operandi in other aspects of his journalism, and indeed with the project of the patrologies, that one wonders, again, to what extent Migne's motives are selfish or altruistic.

Migne's legal troubles did not encourage submissiveness. On the contrary, they only served to sharpen the combative spirit that had led him to want to own newspapers in the first place. And if, as Migne remarked to Dom Pitra, he felt constantly submerged by legal difficulties, some of the frustration of writing the myriad of letters that are now part of his police and press dossiers at the Archives Nationales must have been compensated by the pleasure of offering legal advice to others.

La Voix de la vérité functioned primarily to advise members of the clergy on matters about which ecclesiastical and secular authorities were opposed—as well as clerics who experienced difficulties with their bishop. Aided in his advice-giving by the eminent jurist abbé Prompsault, Migne used *La Voix de la vérité* to even the score in the old quarrel that had opposed him some fifteen years earlier to Mgr de Beauregard. Which did not fail, could not have failed, to attract the displeasure of the Parisian hierarchy. Migne was censured by Mgr Affre on August 20 and October 29, 1847; *La Voix de la vérité* was again condemned by Mgr Sibour in 1854 for advice offered to two clerics who had been banned by the archbishop.[23] *La Voix de la vérité,* "under the apparently very legitimate pretext of defending untenured curés [*curés amovibles*], insinuates clearly that bishops abuse their power in relation to their respectable collaborators [*leurs respectables coopérateurs*]," writes Mgr Affre, who alleges that Migne "does not hesitate to turn to lying with a skill and a perfidy which contrast curiously with his title." Affre orders "to be suspended, without investigation, any member of the clergy . . . who would openly participate in the editing of *La Voix de la vérité* . . . or who would encourage, even by subscribing or advising someone to subscribe, its publication or distribution."[24] *La Vérité* was condemned by the Bureau de la Presse et Colportage of the Ministère de l'Intérieur on June 26, 1854, for an article printed about the Imperial family.[25]

Though *La Voix de la vérité* and *La Vérité* were sold in the mid-1850s, they reappeared in the form of a weekly called *La Vérité canonique, liturgique, historique, bibliographique, anecdotique,* which, beginning in 1861, again filled the need in the moral economy of Migne's publishing empire for giving counsel. Thus *La Vérité canonique* from the start carried a column devoted to conflicts between ecclesiastical and secular interests. We read in the issue of December 21, 1861, of a dispute between a curé and a mayor over the keys to the church annex: "The mayor keeps in his possession the keys to the annex, one for his own use and the other which he gives to his assistant [*son régisseur*], while the curé cannot obtain one, and the same holds true for the key to the bell tower and to the room where the vestments are kept; he is obliged to ask for it from the mayor's assistant, who is not always at home." The priest, who is, he maintains, prevented from performing marriages and funerals, has already written to the bishop and has received no response.[26] "What's to be done?" he asks Migne, who, himself having been the victim of the ecclesiastical hierarchy, must have relished advising the rank-and-file clergy under such conditions of default on the part of the higher-ups.

Often the advice sought involves real estate. "Pierre owned a narrow strip of land," we read in the very first edition of April 6, 1861,

only four meters wide, the length of the parish church of N. Some 50 years ago he built a shed on this spot, and he buttressed his structure against the wall of the church without having received authorization; rather, he gave himself permission, since, at the time, he was himself mayor of the commune.

I am asking: 1º If those responsible for the maintenance of the church cannot, despite the statute of limitation of 50 years, oblige him to build on his own property a new wall at a distance of one meter from the church?

2º If we would be able, in the case that we would be obliged to demolish the common wall with the church, which is very thick, in order to build a thinner one and thus give more room to the church, oblige this neighbor to pay half of the cost?

Response: *Constructors are authorized to undertake an action in the courts in order to leave a space of 190 centimeters between the church and neighboring properties* (Law of 18 germinal year x, article 75 and 76. De Gonez ruling of the Appeals Court, November 15, 1853).

Things which are not for sale do not qualify for eminent domain (Code civil, article 2226.) *According to this article,* says the commentator, *one can only appropriate things that are for sale, that is to say, which are subject to ownership by individuals. Thus, churches, cemeteries, public squares, streets, etc., cannot be acquired by prescription: Nec usucapiuntur res sacrae, sanctae, publicae.*

The jurisprudence of Courts respects this doctrine and has always decided that one cannot appropriate churches, which must be protected from all habitation or construction, no matter what.

There is, then, no difficulty, under the rule of appropriation, which the neighbor of this church cannot invoke since he has dared without any legal right to construct a shed within the legal limit of 1 meter 90 centimeters, that is to say, almost two meters.

One must answer the first question thus: That it is at once a right and a duty for those responsible for the maintenance of the church to oblige the owner to remove his building not only one meter from the church, but 1 meter 90 centimeters.

To the second question. Negatively. The church wall, not being and not being able to be common in the present case, the neighbor is not obliged to pay half the cost: it is enough for him to move his shed, which is placed too close to the church.[27]

Elsewhere, a priest who has bought a house, a courtyard, and a pasture for his horse is disturbed that the local commune wants to destroy trees bordering his land in order to build a school.[28] "What's to be done?" he too demands.

Under the rubric "Liturgical Law" (*Droit liturgique*) the canonical advice is decidedly less earthly. A priest wants to know if "during the octave of Saint Peter and Saint Paul, one commemorates these two apostles by a single antiphon and a single prayer (*oraison*) which is common to them, when one celebrates another office; can one do the same thing during the octave of both?"[29] Another asks, "Can one receive recompense (*des honoraires*) for the three masses of Christmas, as the *De Lugo* teaches (*Cours complets*, tome XXIII, page 847)"; and, still another: "Is one obliged to act as for the other multiple ceremonies [*binages*] and as do the priests of Spain and Portugal for the three masses sung on the day of the dead?"[30]

From legal and liturgical advice to preemptive warnings is but a small step. Migne, for example, sounds the alert to members of the clergy who have invested their funds with a certain M. Mirès of a judgment rendered against him before "the commercial court of the Seine, dated April 4, [1861]." And from the kind of alert which assumes, despite the official source, the existence of a closed community of interested listeners, it is even a smaller step to less official and less formal versions of communal alertness which take the form of hearsay. Counsel elides quickly and naturally in Migne's journalism into rumor and gossip. He informs his readers, for example, in a sensationalist flourish that could only have been aimed, like that of any scandal sheet, at increasing newspaper sales, of a "horrible tragédie" that occurred in the United States:

The reverend George Andrews, pastor of a Methodist church, a man showing a great zeal for the interests of religion and excessively severe moral principles, had succeeded in seducing one of his nieces whom he had taken into his home. The poor girl, filled with shame because of her sin, wanted to end the guilty relations with her uncle, who pursued her unceasingly with his importunate advances; and when she resisted his desires, he carried out the most brutal violence against her person. . . . She sought refuge with neighbors. . . . Andrews was summoned to appear . . . before the judge. . . . Explanations were . . . exchanged between the minister and his accusers . . . Andrews, exasperated by these words, discharged his revolver upon those with whom he spoke; he killed one on the spot, wounded another seriously, and missed the third. . . . Andrews, captured, was soon tied up . . . Recognized as guilty by a jury composed of seventy of his fellow citizens, Andrews was condemned to be hanged as soon as possible. At midnight, in the presence of a great crowd of the curious . . ., he submitted to the fatal sentence. The last words of this wretch were: "I am only sorry about one thing in dying, that is, not having killed three or four more!"[31]

Here we have a splendid example of Migne's journalistic procedure, which has all the earmarks of a rumor-driven grapevine rather than of firsthand reporting. News of the incident, which took place in Sumter (sic) County, Florida, has somehow traveled to New York; from New York someone has written to the *Gazette*, whence Migne merely reproduces the truth and the facts, though at second or third hand. So too, we read that "the State of Texas has been the theater of one of those scenes of barbarism over which the South of the United States, to the shame of humanity, has a monopoly," through "two letters addressed to the *Tribune de New-York* from the town of Buchanan in Texas." What's more, in order to guarantee that the truth has traveled unblemished from Texas to the Ateliers catholiques, Migne asserts that "one would like to be able to cast doubt upon such news, but its authenticity is incontestable."[32]

Under the rubric "Anecdotal News" (*Nouvelles Anecdotiques*) Migne reproduces "for the recreational section of *La Vérité*" clerical hearsay and scabrous anecdotes.

Everyone knows that M. Boyer, a pious ecclesiastic, learned and zealous as few produced by the French Clergy, was the most distracted of men. One day he had just said mass; and, as he was a bit hurried, he forgot to remove his sacerdotal clothes. He took his square bonnet for his hat and went out so dressed in the streets of Paris. . . . One day, he attended. . . . A third time, it was on a feast day, there was a crowd at Saint-Sulpice, and the supper hour having been a bit changed, this was enough to make this venerable distracted man lose his memory. [Italics mine.][33]

Elsewhere in the same paper Migne reproduces a story—told by M. l'abbé Coudrin de Mende to M. Vernet, "former superior of the seminary of Viviers," who has sent it to *La Vérité canonique*—of a great noble under the Ancien Régime who disappeared once a year to engage "in debauchery and the wildest libertinage" (*dans la débauche et le libertinage le plus effréné*) with "a great number of poor people of both sexes," and who was convinced by a friend, under the threat of exposure, to reform himself: "In fact, he furnished him on the spot with clean and decent clothes in order that he might give up his rags, and he threatened him, if he came back again, to expose his turpitude not only to his family, to the inhabitants of his neighborhood, but to those living in the whole region covered by his seigniory." "It was a good and effective lesson," Migne concludes in a narration that resembles nothing so much as the medieval morality tale or *exemplum*.[34]

Editing with Scissors

LA VÉRITÉ CANONIQUE, like the *Journal des faits* and *La Voix de la vérité*, was a "reprint digest"—a "journal reproducteur"—of the type which abounded at mid-century: e.g., *l'Estafette, Le Compilateur, Le Journal des journaux, l'Echo des feuilletons*. As such, it did not so much publish articles written expressly for it as reproduce that which had already been printed elsewhere in the mode of what is known today as a digest, much like the popular American *Reader's Digest*. Migne's journalistic career was, in fact, primarily oriented toward reprinting without change articles from other newspapers throughout the world; and one reads no phrase more frequently in the pages of *La Vérité canonique* than the phrase "one reads" or "one writes": "One reads in the *Italie*," "One writes from Hondschoote to the *Propagateur de Lille*," "One writes from Munich to the *Journal de Bruxelles*," "One reads in the *Gazette du Midi*," or "One reads in the *Gazette des tribunaux*."[35] Nor does Migne attempt to hide this aspect of his editorial policy. He is absolutely without pretension where the question of originality is concerned. "The nature of this newspaper being to reflect other papers (*les autres feuilles*) means that it does not need an editor-in-chief," he writes to the Ministre de l'Intérieur on December 13, 1853 (AN F18 333a), in a paradoxical act of presence which proclaims his very absence. Nor, finally, did Migne invent anything original. He had in his journalistic endeavors been preceded by the famous example of Emile Girardin, who was no doubt one of the models for the journalists of Balzac's *Illusions perdues*, and who in 1829, lacking sufficient funds to pay for an editorial board or even to hire writers, nonetheless founded a newspaper, named with epic humor *Le Voleur,* which reprinted the "best articles of the week" from elsewhere. Girardin used the profits to found in 1830 another newspaper, *La Mode,* to which Balzac contributed, before launching *Le Journal général de la France* and, six years later, *Le Siècle.*[36]

The reproduction of others can be seen, first, as a money-saving measure, a consideration to which Migne was certainly not immune. A police report of December 11, 1853, makes it clear that "this is a newspaper without editorial costs since it specializes in reproducing that which is edited elsewhere" (AN F18 333a). The possibility of the editorless newspaper, part of Migne's instinctual reflex toward hiding his own editorial voice behind that of others, offered, second, an obvious legal advantage of owning more than one newspaper at a time and was thus part of the proprietary strategy that we have seen in relation to the registration of licenses (*brevets*) and the ownership of working capital. As long as no editor is involved, the potential for ownership becomes limitless; the superimposition of the legal fictions merely doubles the procedure of edition by reproduction. Reproduction is, in fact, the prime explanatory image in Migne's journalistic persona, and he associates the urge to multiple ownership with the paternal instinct. "Can a father not love several children? Should he desire the death of one in order to fatten up [*engraisser*] the others? This is the rule of nature," he writes to the stockholders (*messieurs les actionnaires*) of *Le Journal des faits* on November 11, 1853 (AN F18 369).

More important, the legal fiction of the nonexistent editor had the effect of detaching Migne from what he published, which he claims not to have read, much less, of course, to have written. "I am one of the busiest men in France, for my print house is without doubt the largest which has existed since the invention of printing," he writes to the Ministre de l'Intérieur on June 28, 1854. "For this reason I am forced by circumstances to have confidence in several editors and proofreaders. Thus too my inability to read even a tenth of what I print" (AN F18, 333a). Migne thus rhetorically displaces editorial responsibility in such a way as to answer preemptively, indeed to render absurd, the very charges which eventually shut down *Le Journal des faits.* There can be no such thing as "fraudulent printing"—*contrefaçon*—he seems to say in advance, when the very essence of the journal is to reproduce that which has already been published elsewhere. Nor does the notion of false news make sense. For Migne manages through the "journal reproducteur" to detach his repetition of the news from his own voice, and therefore from anything resembling individual responsibility or intent.

Coming from nowhere, like the self-made man Migne himself, the voice of the truth—*La Voix de la vérité*—is unassignable, diffuse, everywhere and yet at the same time impossible to locate. The truth of the *Journal des faits,* like that of *La Voix de la vérité* is thus perceived—through the rhetoric of the "journal reproducteur"—as being completely objective, impartial, universal in its refusal of the particular. "We cite facts, because facts often point to rights and duties," he writes in *l'Univers* of November 23, 1833. "We will give the opinion of newspapers on every major event because the truth almost always emanates from the clash of opinions; *but we will leave all systems aside, because systems divide [mais nous nous tiendrons en dehors de tout système, parce que les systèmes divisent]*" (italics mine). Migne's newspapers are thus supposedly neutral, without ideology, the vehicles through which something like the raw truth, rooted in the abundant reproduction of the particular, will spring, and above which it will reign, abstracted from all petty political discussion. *La Vérité canonique,* Migne declares to the Ministre de l'Intérieur on September 12, 1860, "will contain no substantive article . . . will not engage in any discussion of current initiatives. . . . Instead of leading the clergy in the direction of this or that political position opposed to the government, it will remove the clergy from all opinions by positioning it in a superior realm, the only one worthy of its high mission" (AN F18 283). Pushed to a logical extreme, Migne's "journaux reproducteurs" become, through the very passivity of the medium, the instruments of political quietude. *La Vérité* is, he writes to the Directeur de la Sûreté Générale, "the most impartial, the most moderate and the friendliest to order . . . the newspaper which best follows the social principles of which the genius of Napoleon III has assured the triumph in our country" (AN F18 423).

Migne's newspapers are thus conceived to reflect impartially a higher truth which emanates, like the Aristotelian universal which is an amalgam of particulars, from the imagined faithful reproduction of historical events. *Le Journal des faits,* Migne writes to the Directeur de la Surête Générale on August 8, 1853, "is a paper which conscientiously reflects all opinions [*toutes les opinions*] without espousing any one, which reports news and not rhetorical declarations [*des déclamations*], which recounts, in a word, the history of our time" (AN F18 369). Migne's editorial policy is, moreover, directly posited against the rationalism of the Enlightenment, against contemporaneous positivism, and against the Protestantism of the Reformation. Thus we read in an early prospectus that Migne's publications will "defend [holy books] against all possible attacks, against the philosophical objections of the eighteenth century, as against the scientific objections of the nineteenth." And they will do so precisely by eliminating the individual and the particular: "Here we have a unique example of submission to authority. What power the possibility of universal reading made available by the editors will render to Catholic principle! And what a rude blow will this same possibility of universal reading deliver to the Protestant principle of individualism and the rational principle of philosophism?" (AN F18 1803).

Finally, the *journal reproducteur* turns the very notion of editorship into a fiction. In his poly-positioning of an unascribable veracity of others, Migne becomes simply the vessel through which the truth, unmediated, seems to pass. He is the voice of the truth, the mere mechanical agency through which the impartial universal becomes manifest: "The editor is a pair of scissors," he assures the Directeur de la Sûreté Générale on February 6, 1854, "given the fact that this newspaper is a simple reprint digest" (AN F18 333a).[37]

If Migne represents himself as a pair of scissors, it must be remembered that the scissors are joined to the productive power of steam. Together scissors and the steam-driven press transform Migne the man into a machine for the publication of the Fathers—a machine that never rests, that has not, it will be recalled, "taken even an hour's recreation" from its assigned task of reproducing an unmediated universal truth that at its outer limit seems even to render language useless. "Few long articles, facts not phrases, complete impartiality, the whole press in *La Voix de la vérité*"—so reads one of the subtitles of the voice of the truth. "All newspapers in one" (*Tous les journaux en un*), reads the other. The epigraphs of the "voice of the truth" betray the nucleus of Migne's journalistic enterprise: that is, the tendency toward the encyclopedic, a bias in favor of compression, the pretense to objectivity, the love of the digest or of that which has already been digested, the impulse toward reproduction of what is meant to be perceived as an unmediated truth of which he, as editor, is merely the passive vessel. In the pages which follow we shall see how the figure of the absent editor, as the invisible instrument of a voiceless universal truth which speaks itself, not only occupies pride of place in Migne's journalism, but defines as well the essence of his fabulous industrialization of the Church Fathers.

❖   3

Advertisements for the Self

Napoleon of the Prospectus

THE PUBLICATION OF the patrologies was, first and foremost, the
work of a publicist. The *Cours complets* were sold by subscription,
the conditions of which were detailed in the numerous prospectuses which Migne also published (see below, pp. 80–84). Indeed,
this "Napoleon of the Prospectus" (*Napoléon du prospectus*), as he
was known by contemporaries, was practically as prolific in his
sales promotion as he was in the actual editorship of the Fathers;
and the series of "abominable advertisements" (*abominables af-
fiches*, as Dom Pitra referred to them) which flowed from his
presses are not only monuments to his effectiveness as a publicist
and to his shrewdness as a businessman, but are, again, of a piece
with what we have seen thus far of his journalistic endeavors.

At their most manifest the prospectuses openly sing the praises
of the *Bibliothèque universelle*. But Migne was also not adverse
to—yea, could hardly resist—a certain tendency, which we have
seen in relation to his journalism, toward displacing his own voice,
and thus creating the impression of a discursive neutrality assimilable rhetorically to a self-evident universal truth. Thus, in a broadsheet entitled "Curieux détails sur la *Bibliothèque universelle du
clergé*" Migne speaks of himself in the third person, as if he were
simply reporting dispassionately sanctioned public opinion—in
this case, as it turns out, that of the great French prelates—of the
patrologies. "Ever since M. l'abbé Migne has revealed to the world
of religion the steadfast idea of reproducing the *Catholic tradition,*
universally where authors are concerned, complete editions where
works are concerned, chronologically as to procedure, uniformly
as to format, economically as to price, the majority of bishops
have made it their duty to encourage this undertaking with their
testimony" (AN F18 369). Out of modesty, Migne will cite only
seven. Thus "the most illustrious son of the father of nineteenth-

41

century Christian philosophy, S. E. le cardinal de Bonald, Archbishop of Lyon" writes that "we cannot recommend highly enough to our dear colleagues the editions published by M. l'abbé Migne." An "extract from a letter from the late Mgr Affre, Archbishop of Paris" applauds "a work aimed at reproducing excellent books at a moderate price." Another "extract from a letter from Monseigneur the present Archbishop of Paris" claims to encourage "by my word and by my subscription your theological publications." A "letter from Mgr the present Bishop of Saint-Flour" names Migne "honorary canon of my cathedral." An "extract from a letter from Mgr the Bishop of Luçon" offers prayers for "the prodigious work of your *Patrologie.*" Another "extract from a letter from Mgr the Bishop of Montauban" reminds the clergy of his diocese that they are eligible to receive bonus books by subscribing to the *Cours de Théologie et d'Ecriture Sainte* in twenty-eight volumes. And, finally, an "extract from a letter from Mgr de Gap to his clergy" lets it be understood that no priest should be without "some of the *cours complets* of Sacred Writings, of Theology, of Canon Law, of Holy Fathers, etc., published, at such a low cost, by M. l'abbé Migne."

Here we have a fine example of the continuity—the very uniformity of presentation which Migne praises in the patrologies— between his activities as a journalist and as a publicist. The "Curieux détails sur la *Bibliothèque universelle du clergé,*" a broadsheet coming out of nowhere based upon the incidental—even the accidental, the "curious"—is the equivalent of a "journal reproducteur." Indeed, the broadsheet pretends, like *Le Journal des faits, La Voix de la vérité,* and *La Vérité canonique,* merely to reproduce the voices, or the words, of others—gossip heard on the street, common knowledge and thus received truth, about l'abbé Migne. Which is, in the context of all we have seen, a tip-off to the most curious detail of all. That is, by writing about himself in the third person, and thereby rhetorically appearing to absent himself from that which is said about him, Migne's reproduction of the testimony of important Christian witnesses sounds awfully much like what Migne says elsewhere both about himself and about the publications of the Ateliers catholiques. This is just a supposition, one not verifiable absolutely because of the absence of documents, but still, for all that, more than a reasoned hunch based both on internal evidence and Migne's self-promoting procedures that can be gleaned from the few letters which do survive and that are worthy of comparison with the prospectuses.

In the "Curieux détails" Migne quotes Cardinal Bonald as saying:

He places at the disposal of even the most moderate presbytery collections that in times gone by only the very rich could afford. Thus, the most learned commentators, the most profound theologians, the most eloquent apologists of religion, the most exalted ascetic writers, an entire tradition, so to speak, will pass at little cost from the presses of M. Migne to your library shelves, and you will find there weapons to combat error, and sure rules to lead the souls of the elect along the paths of the highest perfection (AN F18 369).

What is more curious about the testimony of Cardinal Bonald is that it resembles both substantively and stylistically nothing so much as Migne's acknowledged "official" publicity for the Fathers. It demonstrates more than a little his characteristic obsessions— accessibility, completeness (*la tradition entière*) and perfection (*la plus haute perfection*) for the lowest price—*à peu de frais*. Moreover, the supposedly unsolicited letter reeks stylistically of the type of material characteristic of Migne's more explicit descriptions of the *Cours complets,* in particular, the *ad seriatim* accretion of superlatives—"the most learned," "the most profound," "the most eloquent," "the most exalted."

Most curious, however, Cardinal Bonald's letter seems to differ little either in tone or in style from that of the current Archbishop of Paris, Mgr Quelan, who describes Migne's publications as "the most celebrated and the most legitimate in the Church" (*les ouvrages les plus célèbres et les plus autorisés dans l'Eglise*) and who portrays Migne's contribution to the faith in terms so similar to Migne's own view of himself that the reader's curiosity cannot help but be aroused by the quotations contained in the "Curieux détails." "I believe that in undertaking this immense enterprise, carried out with so much zeal and steadfastness, you have rendered a great service to the clergy," Mgr Quelan supposedly writes.

"I believe that I am rendering to the Church the greatest service that has ever been rendered it, and I hope to die as the priest who will have done the most good in resuscitating in its entirety its tradition," Migne has himself written to the journalist Louis Veuillot on February 13, 1858.[1]

The letter to Veuillot is significant, for it demonstrates with an embarrassing explicitness the very process which I have claimed only somewhat speculatively, and therefore hesitantly, with respect to the "Curieux détails"—that is, Migne's concealing of his own voice behind that of another for the purpose of eliciting a positive review of the *Cours complets.* "I have fifty thousand letters of this type in my files; I have in addition the praises of more than a hundred Catholic newspapers spread out throughout the whole world, and I cite among others the *Annales-Bonnetty,* the *Civilta* of Rome, the *Revue* of Louvain," Migne informs Veuillot, editor of *l'Univers,* of which, it will be remembered, Migne was the founder, and whom he would like to add to the series of his admirers: "Whence it follows that you would not compromise yourself in the least in praising in my publications that which appears to you to be praiseworthy." Should Veuillot, however, not be moved by the virtue of praise of that which is praiseworthy for its own sake, l'abbé Migne offers to increase the inducement which has apparently already been extended: "I am offering you again, not two hundred francs worth, but three hundred francs worth of your choice of my publications, if you will only include the list between a head and a tail of your hand" (*la nomenclature entre une tête et une queue de votre main*) (BN n. a. 24633, fol 478).

The cycle here suggested is not only vicious but rich indeed. The piece of evidence is stupendous in the glimpse it offers of Migne's placement of advertisements for himself in the mouth of others. For, one is tempted to ask, if Migne has offered an inducement of two hundred francs—or three hundred at the outside—to the journalist Veuillot in order that Veuillot praise his works, which are, he maintains, praiseworthy because they have already been praised elsewhere, what is there to prevent assuming that he has not done the same, made the same request, of the editors of the *Annales-Bonnetty,* the *Civilta,* and the *Revue* of Louvain? Indeed, it is easy to conclude on the basis of the letter to Veuillot that Migne will take Veuillot's praise, which has been traded for two or three hundred francs in books, and trade it to other editors for more praise; or, as in the case of Bonnetty, for regular good press in the *Annales de philosophie chrétienne* for the publications of the Ateliers catholiques. The potential for such speculation, the playing of one editor off against the next, seems immense, and supports the further supposition that it is entirely possible for Migne to have written to each of the high clergy quoted in the "Curieux détails" with similar claims to their admiration. Or, to hone the cycle just a bit, that he informed Cardinal Bonald of the praises of the Archbishop of Paris and the Bishops of Saint-Flour, Luçon, Montauban, and Gap, suggesting that he, Cardinal Bonald, do the same; and that he wrote, in turn, to each of the bishops with the commendations of Cardinal Bonald and the Archbishop of Paris accompanied by a similar request. The possibilities of self-glorification are almost infinite.

And yet, there remains in the revealing letter to Veuillot the curious phrase—at the heart of Migne's request—to "include the list between a head and a tail of your hand." The displacement of the voice is obvious. Whatever it is that will be inserted will be placed between the head and the tail, the beginning and the end, of Veuillot's own voice, whose representation in published writing is the hand. The question of what "la nomenclature" means is less clear, yet one can assume that it refers to the elaborate list of titles of the *Cursus completus* that Migne has inserted elsewhere and which contains both an elaborate description of the product offered and an advertisement for it, in essence the very praise that Migne seeks to insert in *l'Univers*. Such lists of titles appear, for example, in the *Annales de philosophie chrétienne* with a note in Bonnetty's voice directly following:

The title that we have just transcribed eliminates the need to say what M. l'abbé Migne has set out to do in beginning this publication; we must only add that this is not a *prospectus* announcing what an editor *proposes* to do, but an account of what *has been done,* in part. . . .

Let us add only a few words about the incontestable advantages of this beautiful and great reproduction of the Fathers.

The first advantage is that it is *the only complete one.* . . .

The second advantage is that this is not only *an edition of the Fathers,* but the reproduction of all *secondary works,* of all the *dissertations.* . . .

Finally, one of the great advantages of this edition is that it is very *cheap.*[2]

Again, Bonnetty's description of the patrologies sounds awfully like that of Migne, right down to the enumeration of a series of "avantages," which is, as we shall see, one of the abbé's characteristic publicity tics.

Elsewhere we find that Bonnetty publishes as an insert a sample Migne has obviously sent him: "*A sample of the Greek and Latin type that are used in printing the PATROLOGIE GRECQUE.*"[3] Still elsewhere, Migne is allowed an insert in the *Annales* in which he speaks in his own voice, which is the reference point for the other voices through which he speaks in other places: "Monsieur le directeur," he writes to Bonnetty on January 15, 1861, "allow me to announce through your publication, to the learned or religious world, the greatest and the most fortunate typographical news [*la plus immense et la plus heureuse des nouvelles typographiques*], that is, the completion of the *Cours complet de Patrologie* in 326 volumes in-4o, with 2 compact columns." Here too are to be found an accretion of superlatives, which we have detected not only in the title of the patrologies, but in all that Migne says about them, in particular, the very words (which are here italicized) earlier encountered in the broadsheet "Curieux détails": "Thus, Christian *tradition* is reproduced *universally where authors are concerned, complete editions where works are concerned, chronologically as to procedure, uniformly as to format, economically as to price:* thus is completed the most moral, the most precious and the most significant [*la plus considérable*] publication which has ever come off a printing press in the whole world."[4]

An Echoing Chorus of Laudatory Voices

MIGNE REGULARLY REPRODUCES in his own prospectuses newspaper articles which show the Ateliers catholiques to advantage. One of the longest and earliest broadsheets to survive, for example, contains a long excerpt from *l'Univers religieux:* "The Editors of the *Cours complets* feel it their duty to reprint, following their *prospectus,* the following article. It is an extract from *l'Univers religieux,* a paper no less known for the talent of its Editors than for the purity of its doctrines, and the only religious daily of the Catholic world. But above and beyond what it contains in the way of honorable mention of the *Cours complets,* this article has in addition the merit of making known its nature, goal, means and advantages. It is especially for this last reason that the Editors [of the *Univers religieux*] reproduce it" (AN F18 1803).

That which the editors of the *Cours complets* feel obliged to reproduce from the *Univers religieux* reads very much like—yea, is in places so similar as to be indistinguishable from—the publicity which is contained elsewhere in the prospectus under Migne's own name, the chief difference being essentially one of voice. In the spirit not only of biblical exegesis, but of the patrologies themselves, we divide this material into two columns, the left containing what Migne claims the *Univers religieux* had to say about the *Cours complets,* the right being what Migne says about the *Cours complets* in his own voice:

l'Univers religieux	*Migne*
1) "Here is what the editors do: they borrow, in its entirety and from whatever author, the work in which, according to the opinion of everyone, this author has surpassed all others" (AN F18 1803, p. 17).	1) "For Holy Scripture as for Theology, we borrow, in its entirety and from whatever author it belongs, the best work known on each *book* and on each *treatise*" (AN F18 1803, p. 3).
2) "Meanwhile, in order not to err where the choice of commentaries and treatises is concerned, to give everything to authority and nothing to individualism, to show finally that they work independently of systems, opinions, and parties, what have the editors done? They sent an opinion poll [*lettre de consultation*] to all the bishops, head vicars, theological canons, heads of orders and of congregations, supe-	2) " . . . in order not to allow *entrée,* in our work, to any *esprit de système,* and never to espouse one opinion over another opinion . . ." (p. 7). " . . . we sent last year an opinion poll [*lettre de consultation*] which contained in the greatest detail our overall plan, our reasons, our means and our goal, to the bishops, head vicars, theologians, superiors,

riors, and professors of the Catholic Church, without exception, and they asked them, with respect to each book of Holy Scripture and each theological Treatise, the name of the commentator and the theologian whose work seemed preferable to them, resolved to edit only the commentaries and the treatises which have received in their favor the greatest number of episcopal or theological voices" (p. 17).

and professors of all the seminaries of France, without exception (p. 3).

"We do not let enter into our Cours any commentary or treatise which has not been formally recommended to us! And what's more, only those are admitted there which have received in their favor the greatest number of episcopal or theological voices" (p. 4).

3) "Responses full of insight and encouragement, and that which is even more glorious for Catholicism, responses which reconcile diverse opinions, have arrived from all points of Europe, and have proved that the most celebrated authors are known everywhere and designated everywhere" (p. 17).

3) "In spite of correspondents so diverse in their ways and their languages, we have the consolation of announcing, to the glory of Catholicism, that our great commentators and our great theologians are known everywhere, that they are esteemed everywhere and unanimously designated" (p. 4).

As even the most cursory comparison of the two columns shows, the praise for Migne's publications authorized in the name of the editors of the Univers religieux resembles to an extreme the language attached to his own signature which, indeed, it seems to echo. Nor do the editors of the Univers religieux seek even to hide their sources: "We will borrow here in this review some of their [the editors of the Cours complets's] words, believing that we could not say it better ourselves" (p. 17).

In comparing what Migne says about himself and what others say about him in the AN F18 1803 prospectus we find ourselves in a hall of mirrors in which it is impossible to tell what belongs to his own voice and what belongs to the voice of others. The result, which can hardly be unintentional, is an infinite voiceless regress. For the review of the Cours complets by the editors of l'Univers religieux is itself supposedly based upon a previous prospectus: "Ordinarily, nothing is more pompous than a prospectus, and nothing is more paltry than the works which it touts. Here, it is the opposite: if the prospectus is beautiful, the works are even more so" (p. 19). All of which means that we find reproduced in the AN F18 1803 prospectus, as if it were news, as if it were an objective appraisal of the publications of the Ateliers catholiques, a newspaper article that derives, it is safe to surmise, more than a little from Migne's original publicity for the *Cours complets*.

Nor does the resemblance end here. Migne's publicity for the *Cours complets* is not only of a piece with issues of *l'Univers religieux* contemporaneous with the appearance of the first volumes of the *Cours complets* and of the AN F18 1803 broadsheet, but the very editorial concept applied to the edition of the Church Fathers and outlined in this prospectus cannot be disassociated from the earlier concept of the neutral presentation of a complete range of complimentary and even conflicting points of view which governs the *journal reproducteur*. Thus, the first issue of *l'Univers religieux* (1833) makes it clear that "the editors are, so to speak, on the track of all that is done or is published in books or newspapers or by learned societies for and against Catholicism" and will print "facts, laws, decrees, debates in the chambers and the editorial opinion of newspapers on every major event," just as the prospectus of 1838 maintains that the double-column structure of the *Cours complets* is determined by something like a principle of discordant canons: "In every matter subject to free thought, one of the two columns which make up each one of our pages will be devoted to one position and the other to the opposite one. Both are exposed there in all their complexity, and drawn from the two authors who have best maintained them. . . . Thus, in the treatise on *Contracts,* we can read all the arguments for and against interest bearing loans; thus, in the treatise on the *Church,* the *Ultramontanes* and the *Gallicans* develop respectively the arguments related to their opinion. . . . In this way, each reader, free to choose a point of view, can select the one which appears to him to be the most rational" (p. 7). The editorial philosophy of the *Cours complets* resembles to a remarkable degree that which Migne announced in *l'Univers* of November 23, 1833: "We will give the opinion of newspapers on every major event because the truth almost always emanates from the clash of opinions."

All of this is more than just coincidence, or, as Migne might have maintained, universally shared opinion of the objective quality of his publication. One can assume a web of interlocking associations and interests that confirms what we have seen in terms of the subtle pressure and less subtle inducements exerted by Migne upon editors like Bonnetty and Veuillot. The prospectus contained in AN F18 1803 has no date. We read on page 3, however, that "we sent *last year* an opinion poll [*lettre de consultation*]," which would place it in 1838 since Migne supposedly sent this polling letter in late 1837. We know further that this prospectus must have been issued at the beginning of the project of the *Cours complets,* since Migne claims in his own voice that "the first twelve volumes were on sale March 20, 1838" (p. 1); and on page 19 we read in the extract supposedly from *l'Univers religieux* that "we have under our eyes the first twelve volumes" (p. 19).[5] Migne, it will be remembered (above, p. 24), was the original founder of *l'Univers religieux;* and though he sold it in 1836, one can only conclude that his relations with the editors must have remained cordial.[6]

Finally, if what Migne says about his own publications resembles remarkably that which others say about them, it is because textual evidence as well as extra-textual circumstance point to the overwhelming fact that he wrote it all: the original prospectus reviewed in AN F18 1803, the part of AN F18 1803 which he signs with his own name, the review in *l'Univers religieux* of the original prospectus, the reproduction of this review also contained in AN F18 1803. Migne's journalistic and patrological personae were the same precisely because he managed to multiply his voice uncannily—a canonical echolalia—in a variety of seemingly unrelated publications. The more he was able to place what he delicately phrases in the letter of February 13, 1858, to Veuillot as "the list between a head and a tail of your hand," the more his own voice was displaced to join the chorus of publicity for the *Cours complets.*

In this Migne was apparently in advance of his time but hardly unique. Michael Miller, whose history of the Bon Marché department store holds surprising resonance for our understanding of Migne, demonstrates a similar collusion between the Bon Marché and the press—especially *l'Illustration* and *Le Monde illustré*—in the 1870s and 1880s. It appears that the articles in both journals were frequently identical; they were, like reviews of Migne's publications in the *Univers religieux* and the *Annales de philosophie chrétienne*, filled with "blatant advertising content"; and handwritten copies of the articles are to be found in the Bon Marché Archives. Furthermore, the published accounts were reprinted by the Bon Marché and distributed to those who took the house tour as well as becoming part of the yearly agenda. Miller speculates that the 190,000 francs spent in 1891 and 1892 for "various work in defense of the interests of the *grands magasins*" went to those who wrote such favorable pieces as well as to direct payoffs to newspapers.[7]

Then too, in this case as elsewhere, there is almost no aspect of Migne's journalistic or publicity endeavors that is not also detailed in Balzac's *Illusions perdues*. One of the prime themes of this epic of journalistic corruption during the Restoration is the constant traffic in reviews paid for in one way or another by self-promoting editors. Balzac's cynicism toward the Parisian press reaches an apogee in the famous discussion between the reviewers Finot and Etienne Lousteau in the bookshop of Dauriat:

"By the way, it's agreed that we cry up Paul de Kock: Dauriat has taken over two hundred copies of his book and now Victor Ducange is refusing him a novel. Dauriat says he wants to build up a new author in the same line. So you'll put Paul de Kock over Ducange."

"But Ducange and I have a play on at the Gaieté," said Lousteau.

"All right, you'll tell him I wrote the article. You'll make out I did a savage review and that you toned it down: he'll be grateful to you." (English edition, p. 267; French edition, p. 296)

Balzac recognizes the extent to which commissioned articles of the type which would have been familiar to Migne belong to the regular cost of book publication. Again, Dauriat, "the Sultan of booksellers," to Lucien de Rubempré: "In the last two years I've brought three people into the limelight, which means that I've brought triple ingratitude on myself. Nathan is claiming six thousand francs in review articles and didn't bring me a thousand francs. As for Blondet's two articles, they cost me a thousand francs and a dinner which set me back five hundred francs."[8] The commercial success of books was dependent upon the kind of remunerated reviews that were at the time somewhat of a novelty and no more than a primitive form of advertising attached from the outset to Romanticism:

> Yet another fact will explain the power such articles wielded. Monsieur de Chateaubriand's book on the last of the Stuarts was languishing in a warehouse, unsalable. Thanks to a single article written by a young man in the *Journal des débats,* the book was sold out in a week. . . . In fact the trade in books styled *livres de nouveauté* can be summed up in this commercial theorem: a ream of blank paper is worth fifteen francs; once printed it is worth five francs or three hundred francs according to the success it obtains. In those times, a favourable or hostile article often decided this question of finance. (English edition, p. 365; French edition, p. 413)

Again, this means that Migne's journalistic undertakings can be situated at the very threshold of an awareness of the advertising potential of newspapers: "The influence and power of newspapers are only just dawning," said Finot. "Journalism is in its infancy; it will grow up. In ten years from now, everything will be subject to publicity" (English edition, p. 313; French edition, p. 355). The newspaper as a vehicle of paid publicity was quite literally in a state of infancy, the first advertisements appearing apparently in 1836. Emile de Girardin, a journalist and publicist, the equivalent in many respects of a secular Migne, announced in the first number of *La Presse* that subscriptions would no longer pay for editorial and printing costs, but continued "It's up to advertising to pay for the newspaper" (*C'est aux annonces de payer le journal*).[9]

Migne regularly practiced the sort of ventriloquistic self-promotion that is symptomatic of the fluid relationship between book publishing, promotion, and the journalism of the times. Balzac observes that beginning with the Restoration, book publishers, impelled by the cost of paid newspaper announcements, turned toward the "inserted article."[10] Tyrannized by newspaper editors, book editors resorted to the advertising broadsheet—posters or the visual equivalents of Migne's prospectuses:

> In their resistance to journalistic tyranny, Dauriat and Ladvocat were the first to invent posters, by means of which they could bring their books to the attention of Parisians with a display of fancy type, a quaint use of colours, vignettes and, later, lithographs, thus making posters a poem for

the eyes and often a drain on the amateurs' purses. (English edition, p. 363; French edition, p. 411)

Eventually, however, they returned to the paid announcement, Girardin's "ad that will pay for the newspaper."[11]

The easy cohabitation of the newspaper article and the free-standing poster or prospectus leads to a blurring of boundaries between the supposed objectivity of the press and the self-generated interest of the paid advertisement; and it is just such a mix that we have seen in relation to *l'Univers religieux*—that is, Migne's reproduction in his prospectuses of what had already been reproduced in the "newspaper digests" to which he also no doubt had some input. "Some time ago," he writes in the "Curieux détails sur la *Bibliothèque universelle du clergé*,"

the newspapers *l'Estafette* and *La Banlieu de Paris* wrote: "Leaving the Enfer district [*la barrière d'Enfer*], you will see a vast establishment. . . . If you enter into it, you will find yourself before one of the greatest print industries of Europe, to judge by the number of publications, the size of the workforce, and by the dimensions of the building itself. The main print house is itself bigger than a church. Elsewhere, you will see a series of *small-printshops* in action. . . . More than three hundred workers—smelters, stereotypers, glazers, smoothers, collators, binders, typesetters, printers, mechanics, etc. . . . Walk through the warehouses. . . . They probably are unequaled anywhere in the world: these are armed camps of in-quarto [*des fortifications d'en-4o*]. . . . There is much here to make Guttemberg [sic] jump with joy at the bottom of his grave. . . . M. Migne has thus fulfilled the dream of many a Pope; he has through his industrial acumen and his inexhaustible energy carried off a revolution in printing." (AN F18 369)

One cannot prove, of course, that Migne actually wrote the above article, which he claims to have read in the popular press, though, once again, the exaggerated comparison with Gutenberg, the dream of Popes (see above, p. 8), the interminable lists, the precise contents of those lists, the serial superlatives are characteristic of his self-promotional style. Indeed, even the conclusion which can be drawn from all the Christian witnesses at the end of the "Curieux détails," and in which Migne quotes from his own prospectuses as well as from the text printed on the top of his letterhead stationery, sounds curiously like the passage quoted from *l'Esta-fette* and *La Banlieu de Paris:*

Facts being what they are, it is no longer surprising to read in the *prospec-tuses* and on the *letterhead stationery* of the *Ateliers* of Montrouge:
    TO ALL MEMBERS OF THE CATHOLIC CLERGY.
    If you would like to see carried out *all at once and on a grand scale* all the arts relating to printing, you are invited to honor with your presence the *Ateliers catholiques* of Petit-Montrouge. They are all to be found there. Indeed, in order to be convinced of that, one need only take a look at the words *print shop, bookstore, foundry; stereotyping, glazing, smoothing, collating,* and *binding,* which are on the entrance to the establishment, and which cannot be found together elsewhere, not even in the Imprimerie nationale. (AN F18 369)

Such evidence would be less convincing were it not for the fact that the newspapers which Migne cites, *l'Estafette* and *La Banlieu de Paris,* were also reprint digests; and it is, again, more than probable that the news of a visit to the Ateliers catholiques which they have supposedly printed and which Migne reproduces in "Cu-rieux détails" as if it were from an independent external source was anything but original and either could have came from one of Migne's "journaux reproducteurs"—*La Voix de la vérité, Le Jour-nal des faits,* or *La Vérité canonique*—or could have been repro-duced from one of Migne's other prospectuses, through which it was merely recycled. What seems most certain is that it came at some point from Migne himself, around whom a circle of laudatory voices spreads; with one final proviso: the wider this circle gets, the more univocal it becomes.

Thus the request to Veuillot for "the list between a head and a tail of your hand" can only represent an attempt to publish under the name of another that which belongs in fact to Migne's own voice, and that will, as I have assumed in the case of the "Curieux détails," in turn be quoted in another of his apparently objective descriptions of the unsolicited opinion of others—of ei-ther the high clergy of France or of the fifty thousand letters of praise which he supposedly has tucked away in files. Indeed, Migne claims (or threatens), again in the "Curieux détails," that as soon as the *Cours complets* are complete the letters will be taken out of their cache and published in toto: "More than 50,000 [similar letters] coming from the [ecclesiastical] hierarchy at every level and from all countries could be produced! This unbelievable but true number of congratulations, and those which might still come in, will be gathered in 10 or 12 volumes of the format of the *Cours*" (AN F18 369). The ten- or twelve-volume collection of the letters of praise which Migne has to a lesser or greater degree solicited either directly or simply by apprising other potential correspondents of their existence constitutes a fitting culmination to the patrologies, a self-generated simulated summa of all the good that Migne has accomplished at a fair price—*du bon, à bon marché*: "the good and the good and cheap."

In the beginning, thus, are the letters of praise which authorize publication, and which become publications in their own right. For while Migne may have only threatened to publish fifty thousand letters once the *Cours complets* were complete, he did, he claims in an insert in the *Annales de philosophie chrétienne* under the bold rubric of "**Avis important**," actually publish a prospectus containing some fifteen hundred: "Before sending out a *Prospectus* of almost 200 pages, where one can read more than 1,000 Episcopal Letters and more than 500 from the leaders of Catholicism in favor of our Work, we feel obliged to address the present Announcement to the religious Public."[12] The **Réflexions instructives et curieuses sur la Patrologie** which follow show the same supposedly objective detachment of the innocent reader before the "Curieux détails" which we have already encountered.

Further, the letters are joined by preaching, a verbal proselytizing, of which they are merely the written version. The endorsement of the great prelates of France, induced either by Migne's direct solicitation or by his indirect suggestion that each should vouch in writing for the patrologies because others have done so, thus becomes, in his self-legitimating sales pitch, a topic of predication. Those who preach are obliged to spread the word throughout the land: "In ecclesiastical retreats, by order of the Ordinary, or through his own motivation, the preacher, at the very moment that he speaks with the most passion about the duty to study, rarely forgets to put in a word of praise about the number, the importance, and the attractive price [*le prix minime*] of that which is produced by the *Ateliers catholiques*" (AN F18 369).

Again, when the prospectus is read, the ventriloquistic cycle becomes complete. The priest who thinks others are speaking of the
Ateliers catholiques will in turn desire to preach, as the phrasing
of the sermon metamorphosed into a sales pitch merges with the
very words proffered by the prospectus. Nor is Migne's word limited to the dioceses of France. His message is truly universal, and
unto all lands. Not only have "the cardinals, archbishops, or bishops of Bordeaux, Sens, Avignon, Aix, Moulins, Dijon, La Rochelle,
Tulle, Autun, Belley, Meaux, Versailles, Montpellier, and Soissons"
recently addressed "to M. l'abbé Migne equally encouraging letters," but he is being talked about all over the world: "The 4
archbishops and the 24 bishops of Ireland were gathered for a
council at Dublin, when Mgr de Tuam mounted in his chair and
announced thus the divisions of a discourse on the *Church*" in
which he gives as the third reason for the accomplishment of "the
great work *of the Propagation of the faith* the reproduction of *Catholic tradition* by the *ateliers* of Montrouge and its distribution
throughout the whole world, which has thereby been rendered
feasible" (AN F18 369).

In the communicative cycle that Migne creates—and by which
he displaces his voice toward another, who repeats under his own
name Migne's words or their paraphrase, which Migne then quotes
in a self-legitimating simulation of himself—and in the accumulation of letters testifying to the value of his work, Migne creates a
chorus of voices speaking on his behalf. And though those voices
ultimately are only one voice because they either *are* Migne's own
or are motivated by it, the fact remains that he constitutes around
him a web of support, a crowd of supporters, each persuaded
others have spoken, each convinced his opinion is sanctioned by
that of others, each desiring to speak because the others have
spoken. Or, finally, and here resides the ultimate effect of Migne's
ventriloquistic salesmanship, each seeking to buy because the others have bought.

Migne creates the conditions under which those who read his
prospectuses seek to imitate others, to move with the crowd toward purchase of the patrologies: "Mgr Dupanloup, whose name
itself is sufficient praise, just carried a step further his zeal for that
which M. Migne produces," Migne writes about himself in the

"Curieux détails" as if he were simply an uninterested listener; "he wanted, without indicating any bias against the other *cours complets on every branch of religious science,* to confirm that the series on *theology* should serve as the cornerstone of the libraries established in the 30 deaneries of his diocese. Almost all the bishops of France intend to follow thus their illustrious colleague from Orléans." Then, as if it were the latest news, Migne adds in a note: "In the very moment this goes to press, Mgr the Bishop of Versailles just acted and has opted, in his letter, for 21 publications of the *Ateliers catholiques.*" The crowd of voices singing the praises of the Ateliers catholiques thus was transformed into a crowd of visitors, pilgrims to Migne's typographical shrine: "If you would like to see carried out *all at once and on a grand scale* all the arts relating to printing, you are invited to honor with your presence the *Ateliers catholiques* of Petit-Montrouge." "M. l'abbé Migne is available every day and at any hour of the day, except between eleven o'clock and noon, and except also on Sundays and holidays"—thus the invitation is printed at the top of his stationery opposite the address. The process of accumulation of testimony of witnesses is an important indication of Migne's marketing strategy that takes us in the direction of the innovative economics of the patrologies. For the chorus of Christian witnesses singing Migne's praises is transformed through his prospectuses, which also contain a general public offering of all the activities and commodities of the Ateliers catholiques, into subscribers paying either in advance or in biannual deposits.

Piracy and Patrology

Digesting the Church Fathers

THUS FAR WE have seen how similar the journalistic personality which emerges from Migne's secular and religious "digest newspapers" is to that of the publicist attached to the marketing technique of the *Bibliothèque universelle*. Whether it be a simple sales strategy or a more efficient means of spreading the word, whether it be self-interested or motivated, as the Mignian rhetoric would have us believe, only by a higher good (*le plus de bien*), Migne develops, consciously or not, a voiceless, anonymous, universal persona which seems to come from nowhere and which thus becomes the mere vessel of a universal truth. In the first instance, the "voice of the truth" and of "the facts" synonymous with *La Voix de la vérité* and *Le Journal des faits* is used to hide the underlying truth of the irregularity of Migne's licenses (*brevets*) and of his sources; and in the second, it is used to create a self-generating chorus of testimonials aimed at encouraging a crowd of buyers. What's more, and here we move closer to the heart of the matter, Migne's journalistic practices and publicity schemes are, as we will see in this chapter, thoroughly in consonance with his editorial policy in the production of the patrologies.

First of all, there can be no doubt that Migne did make some small bona fide effort to locate and to publish original manuscripts of the Fathers. Dom Pitra, chief editor of the patrologies, was also charged with the task of finding manuscripts and made numerous voyages of discovery throughout Italy and France. One such trip, in fact, resulted in a historic change in government policy toward the preservation of original documents. Having just uncovered the paintings decorating the beams of a former convent of Templars, Pitra discovered in 1846 a remarkable cache of parchment in the artillery arsenal of Metz. Ordinary paper not being sufficiently tough for the packing of cartridges, it seems that the manuscripts of the cartulary houses of the dioceses of Metz, Toul, and Verdun had been requisitioned at the time of the Revolution and stockpiled for that purpose. Pitra immediately informed the director of artillery of the canonical importance of the manuscripts which were under his jurisdiction for the purpose of being shot from cannons, and he wrote a memorandum to the Ministre de la Guerre as well as to the Ministre de l'Instruction Publique. Within a matter of weeks all manuscripts in military possession were ordered to be handed over to the library of Metz. From Metz Pitra left for Strasbourg, where he discovered the *Clé* of Méliton, for which scholars had been searching for a long time.[1]

One gets the impression, then, from the small amount of evidence which exists to support such a claim, that Migne was at least aware of the possibility of publishing editions from the original manuscript source. A few volumes of the patrologies are, in fact, completely new. The edition of Tertullian was prepared by Dom Pitra especially for the first volume of the Latin cursus; the text of the *Vies de Métaphraste* in the second Greek series appeared in print for the first time. Elsewhere Migne seems to want to make the effort to publish original work—as long, of course, as the price was not too high. In a letter to the editor Dübner cited earlier (pp. 16–17), for example, he makes it clear that if the hard-pressed classicist cannot produce an edition with notes of the *City of God* for 100 francs, or for 120 at the limit, he is willing simply to reprint that of the Benedictines.[2]

In the overwhelming majority of cases, however, it is clear that in making the patrologies "available and intelligible" to everyone, as was his stated goal, Migne simply reprinted wholesale the editions of others. He drew extensively from previously published great collections as well as from selected collections of the writings of the Fathers: the *Maxima bibliotheca veterum Patrum et antiquorum scriptorum ecclesiasticorum,* twenty-seven volumes in-folio, published at Lyon (1677); the sixth edition of the *Bibliotheca SS. Patrum,* eight volumes, edited by Marguerin de la Bigne in Paris (1575) and completed by the *Bibliothèque des pères* (1616); the liturgical collection of Hittorp and the publications of P. Fronton du Duc (1618–24); the fourteen-volume *Bibliotheca veterum Patrum antiquorumque scriptorum ecclesiasticorum* of A. Galland, which supplemented the Bibliothèque de Lyon by adding the Greek and Eastern Fathers (1765–81).

Migne also had recourse to a number of individual or special collections of:

1) Polemics: the *Theologorum quorumdam veterum Orthodoxorum scripta,* of C. Gesner (1559–60); the *Scripta veterum latina* of J. Simler (1571); the *Veterum Autorum qui IX. saeculo de praedestinatione et gratia scripserunt* of G. Mauguin (1650); the *Opera selecta SS. Patrum* of P. F. Foggini (1754–71); the *Opera polemica SS. Patrum* and the *Opera omnia SS. Patrum latinorum* of Fr. Oberthür (1754–71 and 1780–91).

2) Ascetic writings: the *De sacramento confessionis seu paenitentiae historia ex veteribus sanctis patribus collecta* of P. Manutius (1562); the *Paraenetici veteres* of M. H. Goldast (1604); the *Bibliotheca Patrum ascetica* of C. de Chantelou (1661–73); the *Thesaurus asceticus* of P. de Poussines (1684); the *Bibliotheca ascetica Antiquo-nova* of B. Pez (1723–40).

3) Predication: the *Varii sermoni . . .* of G. Florimonte (1556); the *Bibliotheca Hom. priscorum Eccl. Patrum* of L. Cumbdius and G. Mosanus (1588); the *Bibliotheca Patrum concionatoria* of Fr. Combéfis (1662).

4) Apostolic Fathers: the *SS. Patrum qui temporibus apostolicis floruerunt, Opera* of J.-B. Cotelier (1672); the *Bibliotheca Patrum apostolicorum* of Th. Ittig (1699); the *SS. Patrum apostolicorum opera genuina* of R. Russel (1746).

5) English Fathers: H. Wharton's *Ven. Bedae, Egberti et Aldhelmi Opuscula nonnulla* (1693).

6) Christian poets: the *Poetae Christiani veteres* of A. Manutius (1501); the *Hymnodia hispanica* of F. Arevalo (1787).

7) Various collections of Trésors, Spicilèges, Analecta, Anecdota, Miscellanea, Monumenta, Reliquae Sacrae, and Catenae.[3]

The above catalogue, only a partial list of Migne's printed sources, gives some indication of the extent to which the printing of the patrologies was, in fact, merely a reprinting of earlier editions. In this Migne invented nothing new; rather, he participated in a long tradition going back to at least the twelfth century of copying the Fathers in collections; the scholastics of the thirteenth century set a venerable precedant in arranging such collections by topic. Given the extreme rarity of manuscripts predating the pre-Carolingian period, it is hard to imagine things otherwise. The simple fact is, then, that in the vast majority of cases Migne did nothing legally wrong. Most of his republications of already published material theoretically belonged to the public domain, that is, were derived from editions that were no longer protected by the law of July 19, 1793, governing copyright (*les droits d'auteur*), which prevented the reproduction of original works as well as editions for a period of ten years, which law was extended by a decree of February 5, 1810, to protect the author's heirs for twenty years after his or her death.[4]

In some instances, however, Migne walked a fine line between legitimacy and piracy. He was on much less solid legal ground, for example, in the case of the dates of the following editions, which he also appropriated: the *Bibliotheca sacra Patrum ecclesiae graecorum,* published by R. Klotz in Leipzig (1831–34); the *Bibliotheca Patrum eccl. latinorum selecta* of E. G. Gersdorf (died 1874), which also appeared in Leipzig between 1839 and 1847; the revision of Th. Pelt's *Homiliarum patristicum* by Rheinwald (died 1849) and Voigt (Berlin, 1829–34); the *Scripta genuina graeca Patrum apostolicorum* (1829) of C. F. Horneman (died 1830); the *Patrum apostolicorum opera* (Tübingen, 1839) of C. J. Hefele (died 1893); the *S. Clementis Rom. S. Ignatii, S. Polycarpi . . . quae supersunt* (Oxford 1838, Bâle 1840) of W. Jacobson (died 1884); the *Bibliotheca Patrum ecclesiae catholicae . . . delectu presbyterorum quorumdam Oxoniensium,* ten volumes (Oxford, 1835–55); A. Mai's (died 1854) *Spicilegium Romanum,* ten volumes published in Rome between 1839 and 1844 and his *Classici Auctores,* also in ten volumes (Rome, 1828–38); F. H. Rheinwald's (died 1849) *Anecdota ad Historiam eccl. pertinentia* (Berlin between 1831 and 1835); G. Heine's (died 1848) *Bibliotheca Anecdotorum* (Paris-Leipzig, 1848); G. H. Pertz's (died 1876) *Monumenta Germaniae Historica* (Berlin, 1826–); M. J. Routh's (died 1854) *Reliquiae sacrae* (Oxford, 1814–18, second edition 1846–48); John-Anthony Cramer's (died 1848) *Catena Graecorum Patrum in Acta SS. Apostolorum,* (Oxford, 1840); Jean-François Boissonade's (died 1857) *Anecdota Graeca* (Paris, 1832); the *Scriptorum veterum nova collectio,* ten volumes (Rome, 1825–38).

Migne is not duplicitous about the fact that the *Bibliothèque universelle* is, at bottom, taken from elsewhere. Volume 218, columns 368–69, of the *Patrologie Latina* contains a partial list of his borrowings. Moreover, in his publicity he never promises originality, but "the best available editions"—"the chronological and complete reproduction of the first twelve centuries of Catholic tradition, according to the most respected editions" (AN F18 369). Further, the prospectus of 1838 in which he announces the *Cours complets* by citing passages from *l'Univers religieux*—which emanate, as we have seen, from his own pen—comes as close as one can imagine to a confession: "Among the works which we publish, there are some that are so rare that, not succeeding in finding them anywhere, we have been obliged to borrow them [*contraints de les emprunter*] from the Bibliothèque Royale, and to have them copied from the first to the last line [*et de les faire copier depuis la première jusqu'à la dernière ligne*]" (AN F18 1803). Indeed, this document offers a privileged glimpse at Migne's *modus operandi*, according to which piracy is transformed into a virtue and originality into a vice:

It is known that the nature of these *Cours* consists of the complete reproduction of the masterpieces of Catholicism as determined by its living organs; but what one does not know is that the editors fill in any lacunae which edited books contain from time to time with extracts borrowed from other equally important books, and that they do not resort to their own devices except in the case of the strictest necessity. . . . The editors have understood very well that their chief power lies in the older books they reprint and not in new ones that they might compose (AN F18 1803).

Migne's voluntary acknowledgment of sources, published in the *Annales de philosophie chrétienne* when the patrologies were almost complete, takes confession to the self-conscious level of an advertising ploy: "As for *éditions*," he writes in the *Annales* of 1864, "we will recall only that we have given a completely new edition of Tertullian and reproduced for S. Cyprian that of Fell and Baluze; for Arnobe, that of Orelli; pour Lactance, that of Lenglet-Dufresnoy; for Juvencus, Dracone, Sédulius, Prudence, and S. Isidore, those of d'Arevalo. We followed Dom Coustant for the papal letters; . . . the Benedictines of Saint-Maur for S. Hilaire, S. Ambroise, S. Augustin, S. Grégoire the Great, Cassiodore, Grégoire of Tours; and so on and so forth right to the end."[5]

Migne's summary of sources is, moreover, generous in that it unites in one place, like the patristic project itself, that which can be found scattered throughout the individual volumes—that is, the acknowledgment of sources on the page following the title page. Thus for Cyprian (all in capitals, with varying type size and fonts, as well as bold and italics): "S. THASCII CAECILII CYPRIANI EPISCOPI CARTHAGINENSIS ET MARTYRIS OPERA OMNIA, *AD STEPHANI BALUZII EDITIONEM EXPRESSA*"; for Lactantius: "LACTANTII OPERA OMNIA, AD PRAESTANTISSI-MAM LENGLETII-DUFRESNOY EDITIONEM EXPRESSA"; for Jerome: "SANCTI EUSEBII HIERONYMI STRIDONENSIS PRES-BYTERI OPERA OMNIA POST MONACHORUM ORDINIS S. BENEDICTI E CONGREGATIONE S. MAURI"; for Ambrose: "SANCTI AMBROSII, MEDIOLANENSIS EPISCOPI, OPERA OMNIA *EDITIO PRAE ALIIS OMNIBUS COMPLETA, QUARUM INSTAR HABERI POTEST*: AD MANUSCRIPTOS CODICES VATI-CANOS, GALLICOS, BELGICOS, ETC., NECNON AD VETERES EDITIONES, MAXIME VERO AD BENEDICTINAM RECENSITA ET EMENDATA"; and, finally, for Augustine: "SANCTI AURELII AUGUSTINI HIPPONENSIS EPISCOPI OPERA OMNIA, POST LOVANIENSIUM THEOLOGORUM RECENSIONEM, CASTI-GATA DENUO AD MANUSCRIPTOS CODICES GALLICOS, VATICANOS, BELGICOS, ETC., NECNON AD EDITIONES ANTIQUIORES ET CASTIGATIORES, OPERA ET STUDIO MO-NACHORUM ORDINIS SANCTI BENEDICTI ET CONGREGATI-ONE S. MAURI." Then too, Migne never forgets to place at the bottom of this acknowledgment page his own mark, which is, variously, "ACCURANTE J.-P. MIGNE," "ACCURANTE ET DE-NUO RECOGNOSCENTE J.-P. MIGNE," or "ACCURANTE ET AD ULTIMUM RECOGNOSCENTE J.-P. MIGNE" ("Presented by J.-P. Migne," "Presented and Newly Reviewed by J.-P. Migne," or "Presented and Reviewed for the Last Time by J.-P. Migne").[6]

The question of how Migne obtained the editions he repub-lished is another matter. In many cases he bought books that were available either new or used; and a seminary sold him, according to a letter of May 21, 1842, the collection of Galland, which he sometimes reprinted when better editions were too difficult to procure.[7] Then too, Migne borrowed books from the library of Solesmes through the good offices of Dom Guéranger or from Jean-Baptiste Malou, who was Migne's other principal editorial collaborator and who not only passed systematically in review all that Dom Pitra did but also hunted down the editions necessary for the project.

Malou's specialty was the tracking of hard-to-find editions, which he would purchase or otherwise obtain for the Ateliers catholiques to "send to print."

"The only author completely excluded is Nicétas Aquilejensis," Malou writes to Migne on November 7, 1843, "which you cite from the collection of Mgr Mai, but of which you do not know two works which I believe were first published by Cardinal Borgia and by Denis, and then combined in a volume in-quarto under this title: *S. Nicetae, Ep. aq. opuscula quae supersunt duo, nunc primum conjunctim edita, Utini, 1810.* These two works carry the title: *Explanatio symboli; et Libellus ad virginem lapsam. . . .* I just received from Venice a copy of these works, which is in fairly bad shape; it is still good enough, however, to send to print [*passer par l'imprimerie*]."[8]

Many of the books Migne borrowed came from Malou's own library or from the library of Louvain, where Malou was professor.[9] And though it is difficult to determine from the scant surviving documentation exactly what came from where, one thing is certain: Migne was as tenacious in his bibliophilic fervor as he was parsimonious where the economics of printing were concerned. Malou gives the impression that Migne was a taskmaster who would stop at nothing to obtain—and retain—the books he copied. "I will try to find for you the *Epistolae Romanorum Pontificum* in Schönmann's edition," Malou wrote to Migne on February 24, 1844. "It will not be easy. I have rarely seen it announced in German catalogues. I will buy a copy of Coustant this week."[10]

The case is interesting for what it reveals about Migne's editorial choice. Indeed, the edition of C. T. G. Schönmann, published in 1796 at Göttingen, was, in fact, a reedition of Pierre Coustant's *Epistolae Romanorum Pontificum*, published in Paris in 1721. Which leads one to ask why Migne would have preferred the

Schönmann edition. To judge from Malou's letter, it was both more recent and further from the original source than that of Coustant. The answer lies, and this again is just a supposition, precisely in the realm of availability. For, in making the Fathers "available and intelligible" to all, Migne preferred to use—that is, to reproduce—an edition that was less available, or less in the public domain, one whose source would be less visible, in order to avoid precisely the kind of trouble he had encountered in the realm of newspaper publishing: *la contrefaçon.*[11]

What Migne could not purchase he borrowed. In particular, he took books from Dom Guéranger and the library of Solesmes. Here too, Malou gives the impression that Migne was a rapacious editor who distinguished only with difficulty between borrowing and possession; and he was obliged at least on one occasion to require a deposit. "I think that I will end up by giving in to the entreaties of M. Migne for my Ruffin (sic)," Malou writes to Dom Pitra on October 26, 1848. "But in order to insure the return of the volume, I will make him sign a considerable monetary bond [*un engagement pécuniaire considérable*] that I will return to him when he will have returned the volume to me. I believe that the man's interest in money is greater than memories or promises even" [*Je crois que les liens d'intérêt sont plus forts chez cet homme que les souvenirs et même que les promesses*].[12]

A good proportion of the *Patrologie Latine* and the *Patrologie Grecque* was pirated; and the rest, with the exception of a couple of volumes, was either reproduced from other editions or reproduced along with a critical apparatus, which was in some instances also pirated and included only minor additions or changes. Migne often reprinted editions mistakes and all, or he reprinted older or even recently published works without indicating his sources. His dictionaries were sometimes simply lifted without acknowledgment from eighteenth-century works or from more contemporary ones.[13] His friend and publicist Bonnetty notes with obvious annoyance, for example, that the Evangiles of the Arian Ulfilas were merely the reproduction of the recent edition of Gabelentz and Loebe: "We bring to the reader's attention that one finds neither the place nor the date where it was published," admonishes Bonnetty. "M. Migne should never have forgotten them."[14] At an extreme, Migne purposefully attempted to cover his tracks by giving a false origin. In 1861, for example, he published volume CXVII of the *Patrologia Graeca,* the *Novelles* of Leon VI, which he reproduced from the edition of Zachariae von Lingenthal, without, in the phrase of Alphonse Dain, "missing a single typographical error" (*sans en manquer aucun, les lapsus typographiques*).[15] However, since Zachariae von Lingenthal's edition, which had appeared in 1857, was not yet in the public domain, Migne pretends to ignore that fact by referring specifically to older editions of the *Corpus juris civilis.* The editors too feigned a new critical apparatus when they had, in fact, merely transcribed that of Zachariae von Lingenthal's edition, plus a few notes "taken," according to Dain, "at random from here and there."[16]

Migne, the master of the *journal reproducteur,* thus realized in the patrologies a *bibliothèque reproductrice* which was not only produced by essentially the same methods as those employed in the newspaper world, but which affirms the continuity of Migne's journalistic and patristic activities. He had a reputation even among contemporaries for lifting and publishing material that was not his own. He was sued in 1834, it will be remembered, by Picot's *Ami de la religion* for plagiarism. He was again sued in 1853 for "contrefaçon," for reprinting articles in *Le Journal des faits* that belonged by rights to *Le Constitutionnel* (see above, p. 28), while complaining bitterly to Dom Pitra that "these legal proceedings absorb all my time."[17] The Goncourts, who are hardly generous in their satire of the Ateliers catholiques, focus particularly upon this aspect of Migne's character. Not only do the "defrocked scoundrels" and "death defiers," upon spotting a police officer, "scamper for the doors," but Migne "is then obliged to shout: 'Nobody move! This is not for you, but for a case of plagiarism [*une affaire de contrefaçon*]'" (translation mine).[18]

Erasing Names

WHAT ALL THIS suggests is that Migne was able to keep the price of the patrologies so low not only because he paid his workers badly, not only because he drove hard bargains with his editors, not only because he achieved an economy of scale, but because he managed for the most part to avoid paying royalties. The patrologies are, in essence, an enormous theological version in another register and on another scale of the newspaper digest in which Migne, in addition to exploiting workers, rendered those who edited the *Cours complets* completely invisible. He made them disappear.

This is not to say that Migne did not privately acknowledge his immense debt to Dom Pitra, the mastermind of the patrologies, who is said to have conceived the outline of the *Cours complets* in just three days.[19] In 1860, the patrologies almost complete, he wrote Pitra a letter that, again, borders on confession: "I conclude by assuring you that if some of my letters have been painful for you to read, they have been even more painful to write, since no one admires you or has more affection for you than I do."[20] And, in writing to Dom Guéranger, the man who originally arranged the marriage between Migne and Pitra—a marriage that Malou will describe as a "divorce"—the director of the Ateliers catholiques seems to suggest that Pitra's participation in the project is of the nature of martyrological sacrifice, part of the scheme of Christian Providence: "I recognize . . . that our meeting was completely providential. I admire his immense patristic erudition, and I thank you, or rather the Church should thank you, for having consecrated him in a way to working on the Fathers."[21] By this Migne implies that the enormity of Pitra's effort should be above material concern. And though he did pay Dom Pitra, who was always in need of money, three hundred francs for each revised volume of the patrologies and fifty francs for each sheet of the Index Tables, he did, in making such an arrangement, impose upon Pitra the silence of the confessional—"All this in confidence as in the penitential booth" (*Tout cela confidentiellement comme au tribunal de la pénitence*).[22]

The notion of Pitra's "consecration" to the patrologies is, once more, one of those instances in which it is difficult to distinguish Migne's interest in "the greatest good" from self-interest, the martyrological glory that the letter implies rhetorically abstracting Pitra's sacrifice from the exploitation which Migne so readily turned elsewhere to grist. Migne promises vaguely in the prospectus of 1838 to acknowledge those who made the patrologies possible:

All the names, on the contrary, which have served as a frontispiece for the first *prospectus* are the names of the true authors of the *Cours complets*. The idea of the work, it is true, belongs to none of them. The material responsibility for it rests on none of their shoulders; but not a line is printed of which the revision and the annotation is not their work. We will reveal one day the part that each will have played in it; but we can emphasize right from the start that this publication is the result of their work alone. (AN F18 1803)

Despite this early promise and despite Migne's unofficial appreciation of Dom Pitra confided to Malou and Guéranger in letters, Pitra is given scant recognition for his masterminding of the patrologies. His name hardly figures in the 469 volumes of the combined *Cours complets:* that is, once in connection with the annotations of the *Démonstrations évangéliques* (an attribution that may, in fact, be gratuitous), and once in column 338 of volume 218 of the Tables, where we find, mixed with one last irresistible mention of Montrouge—"EDITORES PATROLOGIAE apud Montem Rubrum luce donatae inter quos praecipuus R. P. Pitra, ordinis S. Benedicti."

That Pitra should appear to be so absent from the monumental work which he both conceived and editorially supervised is hardly accidental and, again, is of a piece with Migne's "reproductive personality." Indeed, Migne deliberately suppressed the names of collaborators from the beginning. The contract signed with Guéranger and Pitra provides under article 3 that "the name of the reverend fathers individually or collectively will appear nowhere [*ne sera mis nulle part*], neither in the prospectuses and the announcements, nor in the titles and the frontispieces of volumes." Migne's name, on the contrary, will, the contract stipulates, appear wherever he "judges it appropriate, except at the end of editor's notes, which he reserves the right to identify with a special signature."[23] And this is, apparently, just what happened. "I cannot send you the original Greek and Latin text in good shape," writes the editor Fr. Oehler to Migne in April 1857. "The rest is your business. This is why I do not insist that my name figure in the title: I only ask that you mention in the preface that you have obtained from me a copy corrected against the manuscripts."[24] Thus, the prodigious patrologies, whose synechdochic title is simply

"Migne"—"the Migne" or "le Migne"—are so radically fused with Migne's name not because he did the work, which was humanly impossible, not because he owned the Ateliers catholiques where they were produced, but because Migne the supreme publicist—in the nineteenth-century tradition of P. T. Barnum, Henry Ford, or Buffalo Bill—managed to subordinate all other names to his own, which became synonymous with his enterprise. If the editor of the digest newspapers was, as he claims, a pair of scissors, then the very same scissors carefully cut the names of the editors of the patrologies out of the deal.

What the suppression of names suggests is a diffusion of the editorial voice of the patrologies that is, once more, thoroughly analogous to the displacement of the journalistic voice of *Le Journal des faits*, *La Voix de la vérité*, or *La Vérité canonique* as well as to the diffusion of the chorus of laudatory voices of the publicity tracts. Migne transforms, in fact, the irreducible impossibility of situating the editorial voice of the patrologies into a virtue, one that is figured, first of all, in spatial terms. He insists over and over again that the publications of the *Bibliothèque universelle* are not specifically French, but are truly universal; and that they are universal because those involved in their production come from all over. "Also, there are at Montrouge proofreaders from all nations and in greater number than in twenty Parisian printshops combined."[25] And if Migne seems reluctant to acknowledge his editors by name, he is proud nonetheless of the foreign accent of those who put the accents in the Greek and who, as members of an international team of "correcteurs," read the proofs of the whole. Indeed, he introduces them—through the mouthpiece of Bonnetty—like a ringmaster presenting great circus performers:

The greatest attention is given not only to the purity of the text, but even to accents, something that was quite neglected by the old Benedictines. The men who are responsible for this important part of the edition of the *Patrologie* deserve mention here. There are first of all three Greeks, MM. *Sypsomo, Pantazidès,* and *Dobriadès;* in addition, M. Migne has gone abroad in order to seek out the most famous proofreaders, who are: MM. *Lehmann,* from Leipzig; *Reitchardt,* from Stuttgart; *Sidon,* from Cologne; *Béyerlé,* from Hanover; *Guardia,* from Palma; *Laas-d'Aguen,* from Holland; *Tarlet,* from Bruxelles.[26]

Special billing is reserved for Paul Drach, the former rabbi converted to Catholicism and the librarian of the Congrégation de la Propagation de la Foi in Rome, whom Migne/Bonnetty knights: "We still have to name M. le chevalier *Drach,* the most learned Hebrew specialist who exists, and, what's more, the most exacting proofreader we know."

The editorial team was also international, and included not only Malou from Belgium but also Henri-Joseph Floss from Bonn, Georg-Hay Forbes from Glasgow, Fr. Oehler from Halle, Jean Henri Nolte from Vienna, and from Würzburg, Henri J. Denzinger and Joseph Hergenröther, the last of whom arranged to have conferred upon Migne by the University of Würzburg in 1861 the degree of *doctor honoris causa.*

In his insistence upon the internationalism of his "équipe" Migne seems to suggest that the *Cours complets* cannot be situated geographically, and therefore that they belong nowhere—that is, to no one. He goes to elaborate lengths, in fact, to establish their diffuse universality in the attempt to show that the idea of the patrologies is so natural, it occurs so innately, that no one can claim it as his own. And, to follow the syllogism, if no one can claim it as his own, then the question of literary property becomes nul and void. That which is published by the Ateliers catholiques, like the articles already published in newspapers from which Migne disseminated *La Voix de la vérité, Le Journal des faits,* and *La Vérité canonique,* exists in a *de facto* public domain of sorts, not because the material conforms necessarily to the law, but because it belongs to a shared Catholic heritage. Even if others might have had the idea first, the idea itself is so instinctive that it is common knowledge; and, as common knowledge, it is no one's—that is to say, no editor's or publisher's—private literary property. "From the beginning of our relations with the honorable Société de Saint-Sulpice," Migne writes in the 1838 prospectus, "we knew that it, like us, had the idea for *Cours complets,* and that only the preaching of high learning was able to make it give up a project already under way. Soon, however, our vast correspondance led us to the conclusion that there are few members of the two clergies, regular or secular, who have not conceived the same idea (AN F18 1803).

So too, the naturalness of the *idea* of the patrologies is in consonance with the desire to possess the *Cours complets* in a fashion thoroughly analogous to that which we have encountered earlier in the form of Migne's self-created chorus of laudatory voices which generate the desire to purchase (above, pp. 46–55). That the conception of the patrologies would occur to everyone, joined to the knowledge that everyone is talking about them, translates rhetorically into the conclusion that no one should be without them:

May it Please God that each reader of this *Prospectus* might also shout: "Me too, I have often thought of these *Cours,* and often, by my prayers, I have speeded their execution!" Oh! then we would be overcome with joy, and we would say: "This idea must be natural, since it is so universally shared; it must contain, in its breast, great seeds of fecundity, since everyone places his hope in it, and believes, when hearing it publicized, that someone had stolen his secret and his dreams of the good!" (AN F18 1803)

Once again, as in the voiceless truth of the reprint digest, the truth of the patrologies is collective and universal, seems to come from nowhere and to belong to no one, or to belong equally to everyone. And that equality of possession, like Descartes's notion of the equal distribution of common sense, works to create a vacuum wherever it does not exist.

What's more, Migne's notion of the international, universal, voiceless, communal truth of the *Cours complets* not only denies the existence of the patristics as private property, but it negates implicitly the names of those who have contributed the most to their realization. It serves to eradicate the names of the editors, a negation which Migne, whose signature is, in contrast, contractually sanctioned to appear everywhere, justifies in terms of the deplorable vanity of names:

Finally, one has abused the prestige of *names.* It is not rare to see publications, even religious ones, announced ostentatiously with a long and wide list [*queue*], all diamond-studded [*toute diamantée*] with the most imposing names, without even consulting those whose names appear there, and who don't even suspect the existence of this new undertaking. This is a peacock's tail [*queue de paon*], poised to leave, at the first chance, the jay which has stolen it. (AN F18 1803)

Migne, who elsewhere begs and bribes to "include the list between a head and tail of [Louis Veuillot's] hand," here seems overly solicitous toward the sensibilities of those whose names might have been published without their permission, since the names that might have appeared on the title pages of the *Cours complets* will have been specifically excluded by article 3 of the contract signed with the editors and in which a certain nameless truth of the patrologies is most manifest. This is not to say, again, that Migne ever claimed to have realized the patrologies by himself. On the contrary, he admits that others (oddly enough, the only ones to whom the idea does not belong) did the actual labor. To repeat: "All the names, on the contrary, which have served as a frontispiece for the first *prospectus* are the names of the true authors of the *Cours complets*. The idea of the work, it is true, belongs to none of them. The material responsibility for it rests on none of their shoulders; but not a line is printed of which the revision and the annotation is not their work" (AN F18 1803).

Editing by Collation

IN THE PLACE of individual editorial responsibility, which implies individual proprietorship of literary material, Migne substitutes quite literally the notion of a collective effort out of which the patrologies emerge. Even before launching his prospectuses, before selling a single subscription, he has, it will be remembered (above, pp. 54–55), sent out five thousand letters of inquiry (*lettres de consultation*) to all "bishops, head vicars, theologians, superiors, and professors of all the seminaries of France, without exception" (AN F18 1803) in order to obtain answers to the following questions:

1. Which is the name of the author who has produced the best commentaries and treatises among the following lists, and even, if possible, the best part of each individual commentary or treatise . . . ? It does not matter whether the designated author is ancient or modern, French or foreign, dead or living, long or short, a member of the regular or secular clergy. The only thing that counts is that his commentary or his treatise be in your opinion the best of all those with which you are familiar.
2. What is the best edition of each of these commentaries or treatises?

3. What defects are contained in each of the following commentaries which we believe to be wise to faithfully reproduce? (AN F18 1803)

Migne has, upon receipt of the responses, supposedly collated them in order to determine which editions of the Fathers and which commentaries on the Fathers to publish.

Thus, if the editor of the reprint digest is a pair of scissors, the editor of the *Cours complets* is a pot of glue—more precisely, a community of respondants who collectively make the editorial decisions, which, because of their very collective nature, seem to come out of nowhere and to belong to no one. In a certain sense, then, the voices of Migne's editorial committee of five thousand can be seen to produce that which the fifty thousand voices of the laudatory letters supposedly praise. One can even safely deduce, given the reduced numbers of the clergy in the period under scrutiny (40,600 priests in 1830, 47,000 in 1848), that some of the five thousand editors of the patrologies had to overlap to a great extent with their fifty thousand enthusiastic supporters. Finally, if one also assumes that Migne, who has, after all, promised one day to publish the laudatory letters he has received, is telling the truth, then one must conclude that those who praise the project must also feel that they have had at least some small part in its creation.

Migne managed to produce, once again, through brilliant marketing technique, an identification between the producer and the buyer, who has, even before making the first payment on a subscription, a vested interest in the success of the colossal endeavor to which he has already contributed and which, again, belongs to no one individual, but to a collective voice of universal truth. Migne insists, in fact, that the very enormity of the number of questionnaires is aimed at transcending the particular and thus at forging the general, a composite that is a microcosmic reduction of the universal Church. The comprehensiveness of the questionnaire is thus of a piece with the naturalness of the idea of the patrologies and the internationalism of the editorial team:

And, though the responses of so many respectable authorities necessarily endow our *Cours* with a weight that no work of any individual has ever enjoyed, nonetheless, it may happen that they [the authorities] might feel, more or less, the kind of local affection that is natural to a people, and for that reason they might indicate only national authors, authors who are strong enough to enjoy a great reputation in their own country, but who are not, on the other hand, strong enough to have traversed this or that river, crossed this or that mountain, and thus strong enough to have made a European name for themselves; and, especially given the fact that the Church is universal and that in a publication intended for the learned of all countries, it was appropriate to consult the greatest number of authorities possible.(AN F18 1803)

Migne wants us to believe the patrologies were the result of a poll; hence they express editorially the will of a trans-European universal Christian community; and that community, impelled to identify with them, also will feel obliged, so he assumes, whether consciously or not, to purchase them.

The notion of the *Cours complets* as originless and collective thus held several advantages for the Ateliers catholiques, the first of which was really minimal—that is, to absolve Migne, whose epically self-serving schemes might have appeared venal, of any hint of a sin of pride connected to his persistent promotions of himself. On the contrary, self-promotion is given the moral patina of humility: "Thus we have no difficulty in saying what we think, freely and without fear of violating truth or modesty. Our praise is only directed toward works praised always and by everyone, from their first appearance; it is praise for works that we have not even ourselves selected to be assembled in a collection and edited" (AN F18 1803).

The second advantage, more substantial, is a certain guarantee of the truth value of the contents of the *Cours complets*. An editorial committee of five thousand, in which some voices will no doubt cancel out others, insures a neutrality which, again, is synonymous with universal unshakable certitude. As we have seen in relation to his journalism, Migne's pretense to the truth and the facts is linked to a refusal of the particular along with the presentation in their entirety of a range of uninterpreted opinions: "We cite facts, because facts often point to rights and duties," he writes in *l'Univers* of November 23, 1833. "We will give the opinion of newspapers on every major event because the truth almost always emanates from the clash of opinions; but we will leave all systems aside, because systems divide" (above, p. 38). Migne's publicity for the *Cours complets* is of a piece not only with issues of the *Univers religieux* contemporaneous with the appearance of the first volumes of the patrologies and with the broadsheet of 1838, but with the very editorial philosophy applied to the *Cours complets*, which cannot be disassociated from the earlier concept of a neutral presentation of a complete range of complementary and even conflicting points of view which governs the newspaper reprint digest.

One of the measures Migne has assumed in order to certify the authority of the patrologies is, he states, precisely to remain absent, neutral, never to take any particular editorial stand: "to give no entrée, in our work, to any *esprit de système,* and never to espouse one opinion over any other" (AN F18 1803). In the place of the particular lies the authority of numbers triumphant, again, over the individualism synonymous with philosophy—mere human dissertation, opinion—as opposed to theology. To the five thousand respondants to Migne's questionnaire correspond, then, the unified chorus of a collective unified—and because unified, rendered indisputable—Christian tradition: "There is no longer any question of individualism, or of a mere ringing bell; these will no longer be human dissertations, particular literary, philosophical, or theological opinions; this will not be just one Father, but all the Fathers. What are we saying? Not only all the Fathers, but all the writings of every Father where he treats the same thing! We will proceed in every subject, then, supported by the entire Tradition" (PL 218, col 4).

To espouse the particular over the universal would be, Migne maintains, to discount the theological probity of the whole. His editorial maxim is, in fact, *In dubiis libertas,* a doubt whose myriad possibilities of self-contradiction produce not only freedom, but, as we have seen, truth.[27]

Herein lies a third advantage, which is not inconsequential for Migne's mass-market sales strategy. The voiceless, absent editor's claim to plenitude, which coincides with his encyclopedic spirit, avoids the possibility of offending anyone, and thus of alienating any segment of the market. This was particularly important in the conflictual climate of mid-century which pitted Gallicans against Ultramontanes, either side of which would have been lost had

Migne been perceived to have taken sides. It will be remembered that the Directeur de la Sûreté Générale, in attempting to ascertain Migne's political allegiances, concludes that he is someone capable of adapting "his behavior to the situation," and he is suspected of being both for the Empire and a Legitimist. What the prospectuses show, and the similarity can hardly be a coincidence, is that Migne's editorial neutrality allowed him to exploit maximally the potential of the mass market by appealing to the greatest number of potential buyers and, more important, by slighting none: "Thus, in the treatise on *Contracts,* you can read all the reasonings for and against interest-bearing loans; thus, in the treatise on the *Church,* the *Ultramontanes* and the *Gallicans* develop alternatively the proofs supporting their position, and each reduces to the simple form of objections the proofs of his adversary; thus, wherever it is permitted to support opposing claims, both have their faithful and skillful apologist, in matters of Holy Scripture as well as in Theology" (AN F18 1803). Through putting on the reader the obligation to choose, Migne is not only absolved of the responsibility attached to any particular opinion or side of any issue whatsoever, but he induces in the reader, flattered by the freedom to discern from the integral reproduction of both sides, "the flame of the truth": "By this means, every reader, free in his choice of an opinion, can adopt that which seems to him the most rational, and owes his conviction only to himself. The flame of truth is not held hidden from him under a bushel" (AN F18 1803).

Finally, and the conclusion could hardly be more obvious, that which is conceived to be natural, to have been fabricated collectively, to represent a universal higher truth which is everywhere in general but nowhere in particular, which belongs to no one, resolves once and for all the question of copyright. The neutral universalism of the patrologies justifies ideologically the enterprise of the reprint. Migne, in fact, quite explicitly transforms the act of reprinting what already has been printed into a guarantee of perfection. The fact that one begins from an already corrected— that is, already edited—version of the original is less an act of piracy than an assurance that one begins the process of reconstructing the Catholic tradition out of the best possible building materials: "The Benedictines, like the Jesuits, almost always worked from manuscripts, which was a constant source of a myriad of errors, while the *Ateliers Catholiques,* whose goal is above all to revive Tradition, only works for the most part on printed sources."[28]

Printing for Migne did not mean beginning from the beginning, working from a manuscript, as would be the case in the philological reconstruction of the later part of the century and especially after the Franco-Prussian war. It meant refining what had already been set in print. Thus the emphasis on the process of correction, and not, say, on transcription or composition. "The essential part of a work like this is, one could say, *the correction of proofs*" (Bonnetty)—here lies the essence of publication for the Ateliers catholiques, where book production is more a question of the refinishing of a pre-existing product than beginning from scratch. "To begin with, the copy is most often a printed source, which reduces greatly errors made while typesetting."[29]

The process of book printing in the Ateliers catholiques is, again, of a piece with Migne's excision of the names of those who produce them, both undeniable elements of the attempt to depersonalize the industrial production of the Church Fathers. As we shall see in the chapter which follows, the purification of the names of the workers responsible for production, who have been rendered anonymous, or subsumed in the one name that has become synonymous with the product, merely reinforces a similar depersonalization in the trend toward standardization of production and precise quantification of labor, print, and especially price in the period of industrial takeoff from 1840 to 1860.

❖ 5

Migne and Money

"Economics Begin at Home"

IN APPROACHING THE question of Migne and money, one cannot avoid the proverb "economics begin at home," for the abbé's personal finances show no less obsessiveness with acquiring and saving money than do the finances which, as we shall see, governed the sale of the *Bibliothèque universelle du clergé*. As Joël Fouilheron has pointed out, Migne maintained close relations with his family, and after the death of his parents, with his sister's family, the Delcros; Migne's family ties implied "a virtual bazaar of familial mutual aids" (*tout un bazar d'entraides familiales*).[1]

The Maison Delcros-Migne of Saint-Flour, one of the most prosperous drygoods houses of Cantal, engaged in a regular commerce with Paris. A commerce, first of all, in money. The Maison Delcros lent the Ateliers catholiques funds during what were apparently the difficult days of 1848 when Migne was threatened with the possibility of not meeting payroll; and, in return, Guillaume Delcros, anxious to purchase a country manor in the environs of Saint-Flour, asked his Parisian brother-in-law to help him find part of the funds.[2] But the exchange was not only pecuniary. Migne's sister regularly sent him cloth for his soutanes, pants, underpants, shirts, gloves, hats, handkerchiefs, and table linen. And though one can find no trace of personal vanity in Migne's character, this does not mean that he was not as precise in the orders placed with the Maison Delcros-Migne as he was in everything he did. "Black," Migne specifies in ordering stockings, "I can wear no other kind, you know my size, I have a large calf and a high ankle, only I need them very high above the knee." Migne, in return, printed on the presses of the Ateliers catholiques the receipt books for his sister, who was just as precise about the layout of her stationery as Migne was about his stockings: "Here is the prototype of the bill that you have requested. We were under

78

the belief that you had kept the last plate. There are no changes, except that the column for meters and centimeters should be next to the years, months, days."[3] The double columns of the patrologies were easily adapted, it seems, to the double-account bookkeeping records of the Maison Delcros-Migne.

The exchange of money and that of goods were supplemented by a regular traffic of goods for money which passed through the family in Saint-Flour. Migne bought candles through his sister, who also handled orders for the religious art and objects sold as a sideline by the Ateliers catholiques (below, pp. 92–95). But, most of all, the Maison Delcros-Migne served as a branch office for Migne's Parisian printing house, taking orders, collecting payments, stocking and distributing the *Cours complets* to the priests from the surrounding parishes who came to Saint-Flour to purchase their ecclesiastical robes.[4] To this day this is the only explanation for the fact that a disproportionately large number of volumes of the patrologies are still to be found in the region—the region which, like Migne's family, engaged in regular commerce with Montrouge. The inhabitants of Saint-Flour sent their sons to work in the Ateliers catholiques (above, p. 20). They also occasionally lent Migne money, in return for which he not only paid the usual 5 percent interest, but annually purchased twenty-five lottery tickets from the "Ladies of Charity of Saint-Flour." In 1860 the abbé hit the jackpot, winning a sketchbook, a pair of pink candle-drip rings (*bobèches*), a soup tureen, a small knife, the *Paroissien romain,* and two volumes that he himself had evidently donated to the prize kitty.[5]

"Du Bon et du Bon Marché"—"The Good at a Good Price"

WHERE THE ECONOMY of the *Bibliothèque universelle du clergé* was concerned, Migne's first concern was price. "Du bon, à bon marché"—Migne's dictum comes to characterize the economic aura surrounding the distribution of the patrologies.[6] The intention was there from the start: in the original request for a "license" Migne emphasizes the excellent value the *Bibliothèque universelle* will represent. "My fixed plan," he writes to the Ministre de l'Intérieur in 1838, "is to popularize among the European clergy the masterpieces of Catholicism through low prices and a beautiful presentation" (AN F18 1803). Again, in the 1838 prospectus, he stresses the relationship between quality and price: "We do not think we exaggerate in saying that nothing so perfect has ever come out of French printing presses for such a modest price" (AN F18 1803). Bonnetty insists on the fact that the *Cours complets* is "the only one that is complete," that it is "not only an *edition of the Fathers,* but the reproduction of all the *works,* of all the *dissertations* that are the least bit useful on the Fathers," and, above all, that it is cheap: "Finally, one of the great advantages of this edition is its extremely *low price.*"[7]

The question of price is, in fact, inscribed both at the beginning and at the end of the very title of the *Cours complets*—*Patrologiae cursus completus, sive Bibliotheca universalis integra, uniformis, commoda, oeconomica, omnium SS. Patrum, doctorum, scriptorumque ecclesiasticorum, qui ab aevo apostolica ad Innocentii III tempora floruerunt . . . Editio accuratissima, caeterisque omnibus facile anteponenda, si perpendantur characterum nitiditas, chartae qualitas, integritas textus, perfectio correctionis, operum recusorum tum varietas, tum numerus, forma voluminum perquam commoda sibique in toto operis ducursu constanter similis, pretii exiguitas, praesertimque ista collectio, una, methodica et chronologica, sexcentorum fragmentorum opusculorumque hactenus hic illic sparsorum primum autem in nostra bibliotheca, ex operibus ad omnes aetates, locos, linguas formasque pertinentibus, coadunatorum.*[8]

Migne was a consummate salesman, and the offerings of the patrologies are filled with all manner of sales gimmicks. He is always quick to remind the potential buyer, for example, that the 469 volumes of the patrologies, purchased separately, would amount to over 100,000 francs. Bought as a series, the price is reduced to between one thousand and twelve hundred francs for the Latin fathers, and only slightly more for the Greek.[9] Migne was anxious, of course, to sell both *Cours* as a single package—"The two *Cours* go together"(*Les deux* Cours *marchent de front*). And the benefits for those who "go together" with them are considerable.

For those who take only the Latin or the Greek, the price is six francs a volume.[10] Those who subscribe to both, however, gain six advantages: the first, of course, is that of price, "to only pay 5 francs per volume"; the second, less significant, is simply "to be able to subscribe without paying postage on the letter";[11] the third is credit—extended payment, a version of a layaway plan, "to pay at first only for those volumes which have appeared and been shipped, and to pay for the others only from semester to semester . . . "; the fourth involves shipping costs, where the added advantage, not to be discounted in the primarily rural settings (the *curés de campagne*) toward which Migne's marketing strategy was pitched, is home delivery, "to receive *franco* the two works at the seat of the arrondissement and delivered to the person designated in the order letter"; the fifth, easy payment, or collection of the sums due COD, "to only actually dispense the funds at their own house and without added expense"; finally, the sixth advantage offered the double subscriber is a chance to become part of Migne's shopper's world with all the privileges of future purchases, "to have the benefit, according to what the administration of the *Cours* sends them, of the prices marked in the diverse *prospectuses* and catalogues for all bookstore items and ecclesiastical goods."[12]

Though the conditions governing purchase of the patrologies may seem like a buyer's paradise in which time does not exist, time is, on the contrary, of the essence. For the offers expire: "Beginning in January 1838, the price of each vol. will be raised to 6 fr., even for subscribers to the two *Cours*." And he who hesitates may be lost: "The *Patrology* is especially useful to dioceses where district meetings and libraries have been established, as it is to truly learned priests or those who want to become learned— 200 vol. in-4o. Price: 1,000 f. for the first one thousand subscribers; 1,200 fr. for the rest."[13]

And yet, to judge by the few prospectus offerings still available for the historian to consult, Migne's financial conditions seem to be almost infinitely plastic, the conditions of sale almost infinitely flexible. Thus, though one of the advantages of subscribing to both patrologies at once is not only the possibility of credit, but a price reduction from six to five francs, the discount is even deeper for those willing to pay for the entire *Bibliothèque universelle* in advance:

THE UNIVERSAL LIBRARY OF THE CLERGY AND
LEARNED LAYMEN
OR COURS COMPLETS

on every branch of religious and human science. 2.000 volumes in-4o. Price: 10,000 fr. for subscribers to the whole *Library*; only 8,300 fr. for those who pay all at once, upon receipt of the completed volumes, for those which have not yet appeared.[14]

As we shall see in relation to Migne's other financial dealings, time, for the director of the Ateliers catholiques, was the equivalent of money. And there can be no doubt that he had, according to an elaborate scheme for the calculation of interest, adjusted the figure of 8,300 francs for 2000 volumes, or a bottom-line price of 4.15 francs per volume, to reflect the amount that this sum, paid in advance, would earn over the period during which the *Bibliothèque universelle* would be produced in order to bring the unit cost into consonance with the full retail price.[15]

Nor is there any doubt that Migne turned a handsome profit on the original price reductions. For if the initial intent was to produce ten volumes of the Fathers a semester[16] or twenty a year, in addition to, say, another fifteen other volumes, for a total annual output of thirty-five, it would have taken approximately sixty years to complete the entire corpus. An amount of 4.5 francs invested at 5 percent, which is what Migne offered to those who loaned money to the Ateliers catholiques, would produce 6.42 francs after just ten years. This original purchase price, amortized over a thirty-year period, that being the mean between full disposition of the cash and full delivery of the books, would, at that same rate be worth approximately 16 francs. At the end of sixty years, 4.15 francs would have become worth approximately 65 francs!

Migne's flexible purchase plan foresaw yet further possibilities of double purchase in what amounts to a nineteenth-century version of a pyramid scheme. Thus, if a priest wants only the Latin or the Greek *cursus*, he need only find a colleague in order to qualify for the reduced price of the combined series. The second purchaser must, however, find a third subscriber to benefit similarly, and so on and so forth.[17] In addition to the *primes* which Migne offered for mistakes found in the books he printed, he also concocted an elaborate system of referral for the ecclesiastical bounty hunters who functioned—through procurement of other subscribers—as unofficial salesmen. Thus, "any person who, in addition to his subscription to the two *Cours,* and that which he has procured in order to be able to pay only 5 fr. per volume, will procure a subscriber to one of the two *Cours* will receive *gratis* or *franco* a volume of Saint Theresa"; for two subscriptions "he will receive a complete Saint Theresa"; for three subscriptions, "three volumes of the *Pallavicini* or the *Démonstrations évangéliques,* and will pay only 5 fr. for the fourth"; for four, "a complete *Histoire du Concile de Trente,* by Pallavicini, or the *Démonstrations évangéliques* of Eusebius, Huet, Léland, Stattler and Duvoisin"; for five, "the SUMMA of Saint Thomas"; for six, "he will receive the *Perpétuité de la foi,* by Nicole, Arnaud et Renaudot." And, finally, for the person who brings in ten subscriptions, the eleventh is free, which is, Migne maintains, "a valuable incentive [*un avantage précieux*] for libraries and seminaries where the seminarists or the students can easily get together and thus reduce by 18 fr. each the price of the subscription to the double *Cours*" (AN F18 1803).

As for the question of sales, Migne is extraordinarily imaginative in visualizing all possible combinations of payment and recruitment. Thus, for the subscriber to one *Cours* who is either unable or reluctant to solicit other subscribers all is not lost: he need only pay in advance in order to receive at a discount the above bonus books. The double subscriber receives a double discount: "Any subscriber who will permit the editors to bill him for the entire sum of his subscription by a single and selfsame draft to be sent out at the end of April will have the right, by paying the simple sum of 8 fr. instead of the usual 24, to a free copy, also free of postage, of our *Démonstrations* or our *Pallavicini* in 4 vol. in-4o." But the single subscriber will not go unrewarded: "—and, by paying 4 fr. instead of 12, [he will have the right] to one free copy of our *Sainte Thérèse,* if he has subscribed to only one *Cours.*" Migne is careful to add that these 8 or 4 francs will be collected at the same time as the price of the subscriptions to the *Cours complets,* in order not to cause excessive incidental expense to the editor for such a small sum; and he adjoins a footnote to the effect that those who will already have paid for the first semester of their subscription will be obligated to 10 and 5 francs, instead of to 8 and 4, "in order to offset the costs of this first draft." Time, however, is again of the essence, and "any subscriber who has come or will come along and who accepts these conditions must give us indication of his intentions immediately after reading this *Notice,* so that we might know in advance if we should prepare drafts for 50 fr. or for 200 fr." (AN F18 1803).

One can, of course, purchase separately the above bonus volumes; and in that case, as long as one lives in France and is among the first thousand patrology subscribers to buy at least three, one is eligible for the "above discount" (*aux avantages ci-dessus détaillés*). Subscribers to both patrologies are eligible even if they want only a single volume. And the same holds, in Migne's sales scholastics, for those who are not subscribers to the patrologies but who are nonetheless willing to pay six francs in advance. In none of the three cases, however, will the price of Saint Thomas fall below seven francs a volume—"Dans ces trois cas néanmoins, la SOMME de saint Thomas ne pourrait descendre que jusqu'au prix de 7 francs le volume" (AN F18 1803).

Industrial Modernism

THE PRICE OF the patrologies is not the only area in which Migne gives the impression of a kind of fantasmatic figuring, of a fantasmatics of figures. For what is most remarkable in Migne's complicated formulae for determining the price of the Fathers is the degree to which they correspond to, are merely a reflection of, an equally fabulous calculation of the cost of production. Migne never misses a chance, of course, to represent the epic effort that went into the patrologies. But, more important, what one might think of as the poetics of his exaggeration is accompanied by an equally exaggerated cold calculation of the labor involved. He is not, for example, content merely to confirm the efficiency of the steam presses of the Ateliers catholiques (see above, p. 15). On the contrary, Migne cannot resist converting such productive capacity into the equivalent literally of manual labor, man-hours, or man-years: "Then too, the hand of a monk of yesteryear could not copy in three years what is done in the *l'Imprimerie catholique* in a single minute" (AN F18, 369). Migne was a prophet of progress through tradition, an evangelist who proclaims the future by citing Tertullian: "In this world anxious for Progress, we offer the Tradition of the past in order to march forward. *Traditio tibi praetendetur auctrix* (Tert., *de Coron. milit.,* cap. 4)."[18]

Though Migne's conversion of one mechanical minute into the equivalent of three years of manual labor may or may not be accurate, it bears witness nonetheless to the degree to which the Ateliers catholiques served as a catalyst to a certain kind of industrial modernism based upon the principle of compression, which haunts almost all he did.

Migne's industrial modernism implies, first, a constriction of physical space. The ordering of information which the patrologies, and especially the Index Tables, make possible, opens a shortcut to the study of the Christian past. And Migne, the explorer who has found a shorter route, has, in the tradition of nineteenth-century historicism, made the world a smaller place: "In effect, one can no longer be frightened in looking at these masses of volumes; one can no longer say: Who can fathom these depths? . . . Thanks to our Tables, these great Series are rendered small; distances are closer together, the first and the last volumes touch" (*PL* 218, col. 4). We have seen that Migne compares himself to Hercules, his publications to the tunnel blasted through Mount Cenis; he has literally moved mountains, or rather, he has cut mountain passes and made, in keeping with Biblical rhetoric, "the rough places plane and the crooked places straight": "Our Tables have carved out a way; they have leveled mountains and rendered straight the most tortuous paths; one only need consult them. The study of the Holy Fathers has suddenly become as easy, as short, as reliable as that of a Dictionary" (*PL* 218, col. 4). In the geographic reduction implicit to the *Cours complets,* Christian tradition, moving now along a straight line, the shortest distance between two points, has simply become more efficient, such efficiency, again, thoroughly in keeping with the nineteenth-century dictionary spirit of Littré and Larousse.

If the *Cours complets* represent a spatial shrinking, they also imply, and here the point is obvious in the easy step from the distillation of three years' work of the monk into the minute of the steam press, a temporal condensation as well: "It reduces," we read in the portion of the 1838 prospectus supposedly written by the editors of *l'Univers religieux*, "the time necessary for research by uniting in a well circumscribed framework a multitude of works that scholars on their own would hardly have been able to know after an entire lifetime of study, and which they would not have been able to find even in the most extensive library, at least in their entirety" (AN F18 1803). The printing presses of the Ateliers catholiques literally compress the effort involved in knowing Christian tradition. They enable a mechanical advantage compared, in the Introduction to the Tables (*PL* 218, col. 4), to that of a wine press: "Our *Patrology* . . . has been in some profound sense squeezed and pressed like the grape under a press from which the least drop of precious liqueur could not escape."

Migne worked an economy both of space and of time. "Who," he asks, "will ever be able to find the time to study all these Fathers, and to read their writings of every kind?" And his answer, surprising in its deference to a world of technology other than that of printing, points in the direction of a modernism that is, as we shall see, the very essence of the industrialization of mid-century. "What an economy of time! It's better than the railroad, and even the balloon, it's electricity! [*Quelle économie de temps! c'est plus que le chemin de fer, et même le ballon, c'est l'électricité!*]" (*PL* 218, col. 4).

Such a reduction of time and space translates ultimately into an increase in the efficiency of faith. From the collection of the Fathers made accessible in one place comes their collective truth: "First of all, it cuts short all that is said against commentary and against theology; for, once our project is completely finished, who would dare to criticize that which everyone admires?" (AN F18 1803). And from such unified truth comes renewed authority: "How pleasant it will be for a Theologian, a Polemicist, a Preacher, a Professor, etc., to see with one look all that the Holy Fathers have written on this or that particular subject! With what facility, with what joy will he immediately find in his hands various texts having to do with the matter he treats and which shores it up! What authority will his words not then have!" (*PL* 218, col. 4).

Migne's version of modernist industrial efficiency rests at bottom on the possibility of quantification, and, in particular, on a quantification of labor. In excusing the delay in the appearance of the index of the *Patrologie latine,* for example, he is not content merely to extol the enormity of the task—"the immensity of such a work, the unbelievable difficulties." He also seeks to describe in quantitative terms exactly what such labor involves: "In effect, we offer TWO HUNDRED AND THIRTY-ONE TABLES for our Cours de *Patrologie latine,* which is 217 volumes strong. In order to compile EACH ONE of these tables, it was necessary to read and reread EACH ONE of these 217 volumes from beginning to end; and this operation was necessarily done 231 times, which yields an analysis of more than 50,000 volumes of our format." Unlike the case of the medieval monk, for whom time—the *tempus* of the secular world—would have had little meaning, labor for Migne is almost automatically converted into time. And the estimation of work is quickly converted into what seems like a delirious calculation of the man-hours required: "Let's assume that a man would have a sufficiently quick judgment, a sufficiently reliable eye, a sufficiently vast intelligence to analyze one of our volumes in fifteen days' time; he would need more than 1800 years in order to do what we have done in just a few years. In order to accomplish this, we have directed to this task more than fifty men for more than ten years, and the result has been obtained" (*PL* 218, col. 1).

Nor, in Migne's thought, is the calculation of time ever very far from that of money. Indeed, his calculations of time are instantly converted into cost, just as labor is converted into time:

What can we say about the enormous expense we were put to? More than fifty men working on the tables for more than ten years, and with only the small salary of 1,000 francs a year per man, makes more than 500,000 francs, without even counting the cost of printing. (*PL* 218, col. 4)

What this suggests is that Migne's contribution consists only in part in the reconstitution of a theological library at the great moment of Catholic renewal. For alongside the actual publication of the Fathers there lurks a fundamental rethinking of the means of such production which assumes the possibility of a precise conversion between time, labor, and price, or between income and cost.

CEO of the *Cours complets—PDG des Patrologies*

FAR FROM HIS role as a simple curé de campagne, Migne gives the impression that the figure of the chairman of the board of the patrologies lurks just below the surface of their doctrinal spirit. He often appears like one of the captains of industry responsible for the economic takeoff of mid-century. Where publishing is concerned, his metaphors are frequently drawn, in fact, from the realm of heavy industry, metallurgy in particular. He makes much of the fact that special letters have been created, smelted for the purpose of printing the patrologies; and we shall see the extent to which both Migne and Bonnetty conceive of the *Cours complets* in terms of heavy metal protection, the plate armor of Christian tradition. The printing of the Fathers, which is in essence a reprinting, is conceived along the lines of the distillation of a chemical or the refinement of a precious metal. The books of the Ateliers catholiques thus pass through a series of increasingly subtle steps in which printing becomes synomymous with the elimination of impurities. Publication is assimilable to correction; and correction, to purification:

By means of proofreaders with on-the-job training and whose typographical eye is merciless where errors are concerned, we begin by preparing a full-length copy without omitting a single word. One reads a first proof against this copy. Then one reads a second the same way, against the first. Then the same thing with the third against the second, and the fourth against the third. We repeat the same operation with the fifth against the fourth. These comparisons have as a goal to see if any of the errors indicated to the office by the proofreaders in the margins of the proofs have escaped those who correct them on the marble and metal. After these five complete readings, each verified against the next, and in addition to the preparations mentioned above, comes a revision, and often two or three; then one makes the stereotypes. The plates having been made, the purity of the text having been captured, one does a final proofreading from one end to the other against the copy, one does a new revision, and the printing only comes after these innumerable precautions.[19]

The end point of the entire process is, of course, and this is in keeping with the industrial revolution of the July Monarchy and the first part of the Second Empire, the production of a standardized mass-produced object to be sold at the lowest price to the greatest possible market.

The books of the Ateliers catholiques are uniformly printed according to uniform rule. Migne is, in fact, obsessed by standards, equivalences, measures, which are not only intended to impress the readers of his prospectuses, but hold the key to his industrialization of the Fathers. The mass production of the Ateliers catholiques, like that of any other industry of the time, would be unthinkable without the type of precise easy conversion between time, labor, and money that Migne the capitalist so potently effects. And his delirious calculation of the labor represented by the patrologies, of the production cost of each unit, of the price that it will bring at the present moment, of the income that future production will generate if the money is received in advance, is aimed in a very explicit way at actualizing the mass production and mass marketing of a standardized object, evident even in the question of the typography of the *Cours complets*. For even if the patrologies did not purport to be original editions, they were, Migne maintains, typographically innovative, and such originality serves as a guarantee of quality:

In order to leave nothing to chance, . . . here, all at once, is the standard and the guarantee which those who have not seen our volumes can expect. First of all, our type characters are completely new and molded especially for us; they are not used for the setting of any other work. The premier foundry of the capital, that of M. Didot, has been engaged in order to make them. The paper comes out of the factories of the Marais, near Coulommiers (Seine-et-Marne), that is to say, out of the paper factory that is the most famous for the meticulous care that governs its manufacture, and it is in the *jésus* format, of the size of an in-8o or rather in-4o.[20]

The patrologies are typographically new. But, more important than the actual type and layout, what Migne refers to as his "typographical revolution" (*révolution typographique*), their originality resides in the degree to which the printed object itself is standardized, its elements measured right down to the individual character, turned out to uniform, quantifiable measure.

In Migne's conception of the books produced by the Ateliers catholiques even the pleasure of reading—visual comfort—was joined to the most exact calculation of the least element of print: "Finally, our volumes are printed in two columns so that reading them will not be tiring. Each page contains 108 lines of 38 letters each, which makes 4,180 letters on each page, 66,880 on each sheet, and 2,508,000 in each volume" (AB F18 1803). One can reasonably assume, and the assumption is hardly out of keeping with the amount of labor necessary to produce the famous Tables, that Migne was also capable of calculating—indeed, the figures could not have not at some point entered his consciousness—not only the price of each unit (with or without discount), the profit generated by each unit (based both on advance payment and payment over time), and the cost of each unit, but also the cost, the price, and the profit emanating from each page, column, line, and letter of the "Cours complet de Patrologie ou Bibliothèque universelle." The writings of the Fathers are, finally, convertible by the quantitative measures of production costs—labor and time— to Migne's elaborate calculations of price.

Again, the fantasy of Migne's precision, or the precision of his fantasy, serves to consolidate the alliance, to create the criteria of conversion, between time, labor, and money that go hand-in-hand with—indeed are necessary to—the industrial revolution of the period 1840 to 1860. The Ateliers catholiques are, above all, a bibliographical assembly line capable of producing a standardized product at minimal cost for mass consumption. It is not, then, simply that Migne's mission in making a theological library "available to and readable by all" can be seen in the pastoral context of the recapture, in keeping with the Renouveau catholique of mid-century, of souls lost at the time of the Revolution, but the very "accessibility and intelligibility" coupled with low prices contain the essence of production according to an economy of scale, a strategy based upon extensive sale of low-cost individual standardized units.

If Migne's industrialization of the Fathers signals a fundamental change in the means of book production, and if that change is synonymous with their commodification, the Ateliers catholiques also changed the traditional means of selling that commodity. "It was a revolution for bookstores," writes Dom Cabrol, Pitra's biographer, referring to the question of price, "the complete works of the Fathers have been made available to the purse of a simple country priest."[21] But the bookstore revolution was not merely a matter of price; the Ateliers catholiques also altered the means of book distribution. When Bonnetty, for example, insists that never was such a thing as the *Bibliothèque universelle* seen in bookstores ("c'est ce qui jamais ne s'était vu en librairie") he refers both to the books themselves and to Migne's sales technique.[22] For the low prices of the patrologies are only partially ascribable to the economies of scale made possible by mass production. They were also occasioned by the fact Migne sold books by subscription directly to the consumer, thus eliminating the middleman. All of Migne's sales schemes are, finally, the very essence of wholesale.

Concern over the impact of the Ateliers catholiques upon the retail book market was a consideration at the time Migne applied for a print license, since this request, in his brother Etienne's name, gives, among other justifications, the one that by "only selling works made or edited by my brother and by me, I can cause no direct harm [*aucun préjudice direct*] to the booksellers of Paris, nor in the Provinces" (AN F18 1803). Yet, Migne's marketing techniques were, along with the accusations of plagiarism, a constant source of legal trouble. Indeed, the booksellers of Paris, understandably threatened by the offerings of direct discount sales, sought help from the Archbishop of Paris, Mgr Quélen, who, in the words of Barbier, "gave in to the greedy jealousies of the bookstore owners." Not only did the Archbishop try to close the Ateliers catholiques—"he thought it his obligation to forbid M. Migne from continuing his work"—but he did so, Barbier claims, by citing canons on a passage from Saint Paul condemning commerce.[23] Migne, however, was not defenseless, for Barbier, taking up the canonical gauntlet on his behalf, maintains this condemnation is legally unsound because: 1) the canon cited was written prior to the invention of printing; 2) Paul had in mind the condemnation "of profane commerce, not a commerce which has as its goal the propagation of Catholic doctrine"; and 3) the licenses for both Migne's print shop and bookstore are technically registered not in his, but in his brother's, name.[24]

Nor, apparently, did Migne ever cede on any point to anyone; and the question of commerce was certainly no exception. On the contrary, when Migne, whose steadfastness derives, as we saw earlier, from an original formative confrontation with the ecclesiastical hierarchy, refused to cease publication, Mgr Quélen reversed his doctrinal stand and, several months before his death, suggested that the diocese might take over the Ateliers catholiques. He proposed "to convert this individually owned speculation into one of the works of the diocese, of which he, M. de Quélen, would be the superior of M. Migne, the director."[25] Migne, "who did not fancy at all" (Barbier) this proposition, again refused, was suspended, and treated as a "priest unrecognized by the diocese of Paris." He was prohibited by Mgr Quélen from saying mass in Paris and henceforth officiated in Versailles, where he was welcomed by Mgr Gros. Barbier is also quick to point out that Migne would himself have been placed on the index—"interdit"—were it not for the fact of his being officially attached to the diocese of Orléans and not to that of Paris. Quélen's successor, Mgr Affre, who, it will be remembered, twice condemned La Voix de la vérité, continued the attempted hostile takeover of the Ateliers catholiques; but, recognizing Migne's steadfast independence, eventually lifted the interdiction, on November 10, 1847.[26] Mgr Affre's successor, Mgr Sibour, is on record as having ordered 5,000 francs worth of books from the Ateliers catholiques and having used them to print an edition of the Actes de l'Eglise de Paris.

Churchly Kitsch

MIGNE'S TRANSFORMATION OF the means of book manufacture, implying the mass production of standardized units, along with innovative means of distribution, based upon widespread direct distribution at low prices, found an esthetic analogue in yet another entrepreneurial project—the fabrication and sale of what can only be imagined to be a whole panoply of kitsch religious objects. For while the Ateliers catholiques were primarily a "workshop" for the printing and binding of books, they also contained what Migne refers to as his "museum" from which paintings, statues, altarpieces, organs, "stations of the cross," and religious paraphernalia of all sorts were sold, also "at moderate prices."[27] "The *Ateliers catholiques* undertakes to fabricate all kinds of religious paintings at the lowest possible price and in a manner worthy of religion" (BN n. a. 24633, fol. 478), we find at the top of one of the many letterheads of the stationery for the *Bibliothèque universelle*. And if the model for the production of the patrologies was that of the medieval scriptorium or the cathedral building site, the model for the design and execution of Migne's religious art was that of the artist's or sculptor's studio in which apprentices work under the supervision of a master, who wasin this case none other than Joachim Issartier, a minor painter admired by Louis-Philippe, also from Cantal.[28]

Like Arnoux from Flaubert's *Education sentimentale*, Migne the "art dealer" praises the quality and the durability of his merchandise:

STATIONS OF THE CROSS

Made up of paintings of which there are few in existence, even in cathedrals, painted by hand in oil on canvas, by accomplished artists, with frames in wood and oil-base gold leaf, a gilding that is not affected by humidity. (BN n. a. 24633, fol. 478)

Migne reveals in the realm of esthetics the same obsessions that we have seen in relation to the patrologies. The first consideration in purchasing works of art is, of course, the relationship of quality and price: "If one wants *Stations of the Cross* at a lower price, one could find them, but neither the material or the manufacture could be as serious," he asserts (BN n. a. 24633, fol. 478).[29] Quality, however, quickly elides with quantity, as Migne the art dealer applies to esthetics the very same principles of quantification and price that are evident in the realm of book printing; thus one buys art from the Ateliers catholiques "sur mesure":

Dimensions and Price
paintings and frames included

Height		Width	Price
0m72c	by	0m60c	480fr.
0 85		0 72	600
0 96		0 79	750
1 10		0 99	940

[etc.] (BN n. a. 24633, fol. 478)

Further, as we have seen in relation to the patrologies, the conditions of sale and delivery of the products of Migne's religious shopper's world become the subject of a minute calculation which leaves nothing to chance: "Case, cross, bolts, rings, cord, packing and collection of sum due at the expense of the seller. Transport only, because of the difference between distances, at the expense of the buyer, at a rate of 13 c. per 100 kilogr. for each 4 kilom."

In the merchandising of religious paintings, Migne clearly does not opt for the unique masterpiece which defines artistic value in the larger art world; rather, he sells by the square centimeter, price tied neither to the personality of the artist nor to the subject and esthetic quality of his work, but to the size of canvas and frame. Thus, the traffic in art of the Ateliers catholiques demonstrates the same traits of style we have seen in Migne's journalistic, publicist, and patrological endeavors: a tendency to diminish the role of individual agency and an emphasis on the impersonal collective nature of production, an obsession with quantification and calculation that transforms the salable object into a standard unit available to the largest possible audience at the lowest price. By his own account, in fact, price hovers at the very limit of esthetics, morality, and economy: "the prices announced are at the last limit of the beautiful and the good at a good price [*la dernière limite du beau et du bon à bon marché*]" (BN n. a. 24633, fol. 478). Again, where the *Bibliothèque universelle du clergé* joins the "good to the good price," the traffic in kitsch religious objects pushes the limits of the good, the beautiful, and the affordable.

Migne's esthetic taste was not always indisputable, however. A painting commissioned, no doubt through the intervention of his brother-in-law, by the Tribunal de Commerce de Saint-Flour did not meet with their approval: "They find it fairly good, but they notice nonetheless certain defects," writes Guillaume Delcros. Migne's reaction, like that he shows before the complaints of the parents of the children of Saint-Flour who went to work for him in Paris, is to question the judgment of those who live in the provinces: "Those who judge," Migne responds, "are neither artists nor amateurs. Christ is rendered according to the laws of true perspective."[30]

Mass Traffic

THE SALE OF religious art was not Migne's only spiritual sideline, for he also engaged in—rather, was caught at—an illegal traffic in masses at several points in his thirty-year publishing career. That is, Migne not only used the numerous brochures he published to recruit workers, some of whom were on the index, to the Ateliers catholiques, but he used them to alert those dioceses of post-Revolutionary France which lacked a sufficient number of priests to sing mass regularly that his good offices might also serve "to centralize" masses distributed either to those working for him or to his subscribers. Migne, it seems, collected, according to accounts—and it must be remembered that such accounts are, because of the illicit nature of the commerce, difficult to come by— one franc and twenty-five centimes for each mass sung. Yet, the priest who had actually performed was reimbursed considerably less than the sum Migne had collected. There were, it seems, at least two means of payment: he would either pay sixty-five centimes to the priest who had sung mass, supplying the remainder in books whose price was reckoned at the highest end of the scale, that is to say, without discount, Migne thus accruing approximately 30 percent of the remaining sixty centimes;[31] or, he would simply pay the priest in volumes of the Bibliothèque universelle.

Such seems to have been the modus operandi of such traffic from the beginning, as we read in the 1838 prospectus announcing the project of the Cours complets:

If, however, the reader of this Prospectus cannot sufficiently acquit himself of all the masses in his parish, or of those that come to him from his friends, the administration of the *Cours* will willingly receive the surplus; it would even by way of gratitude give to the priest who would send referrals its way, one half of a *Cours* for 250 masses, a whole *Cours* for 500, and both *Cours* for 1000. (AN F18 1803)

Should the priest working for Migne's central mass service prefer other works, he is willing to provide instead exactly the same volumes that, it will be recognized, were offered elsewhere as bonuses to multiple subscribers or to those who brought in subscriptions:

If he would prefer, the editors are in a position to give him the 4 *Démonstrations, Pallavicini* and *Sainte Thérèse* for 240 masses; the *Summa* and the *Perpétuité de la foi* for 260; these five works altogether for 500; finally two times these five works or two times the same *Cours*. (AN F18 1803)

However, in the case that none of these offers appeal, Migne is willing—and here the arrangement becomes so slippery as almost to evade historical recuperation—to negotiate with the officiating priest, to tailor the arrangement to suit the individual: "In the case in which other combinations than these would better suit the reader, the administration would consent to do all in its power to take his wishes into consideration." No deal is too small or too large to be accommodated: "and even if he cannot attain the smallest number of masses outlined here, or if it is his fortune to surpass the highest figure, the editors will tailor their appreciation to the slightness as to the fullness of the referral."

Migne clearly realized that the activity of selling masses, or rather exchanging them for pious books, which served as a form of currency between work performed and remuneration received, was not entirely within the canonical pale. The 1838 prospectus which makes the original offer shows an unmistakable self-defensive trait, combining perhaps personal reluctance with the specter of official sanction. Migne suggests, as elsewhere, that the ends justify the means—or the ends justify the Mignes—and indeed serve to overcome the more repulsive aspects of such a mass appeal: "It is painful for the editors to enter into such details, but who does not know that, in order to do good, one often has to resolve to conquer more than a little reluctance?" Further, the need is so overwhelming that even the embarrassing public nature of the offer is to be excused: "The prayers addressed to them by the little people of the sanctuary are so numerous and so insistent that, not being able to respond all alone to so many vows, they are forced to have recourse to somewhat public resources in order to fulfill almost universal needs." On the contrary, the very openness of Migne's proposition is a guarantee against the charge of simony.[32] "The rules of the most rigid theology are thus completely safe here. The masses, moreover, having only been placed into good hands, will be said, well said, promptly said; as a consequence, the conscience of a priest, like the heart of a pastor, must rest easy."

A police report of February 1854 notes the scandal attached to Migne's dealing in masses: "He has engaged in a scandalous traffic, which consists of having masses for the dead said in Belgium at a cost 75c, and of having his dupes pay for them to the tune of 1 f. 50 and 2 francs. He has even offered bonuses consisting of the works of his bookstore" (AN F18 333a). The practice did not escape the attention of the Goncourts:

This abbé engages in one form of commerce that is superimposed upon the other. He has himself paid for a part of his books by curés in the form of coupons for masses [bons de messes], which are signed off for by the bishop. It costs, all in all, 8 sous; he resells them for 40 sous in Belgium, where there aren't enough priests to fulfill all the endowments of masses established at the time of the Spanish domination. . . . A purse full of masses![33]

Nor, finally, did it elude the ecclesiastical hierarchy. Migne, who, it will be remembered, had at one point been barred from conducting mass in Paris, was suspended by the Archbishop of Paris in 1874 for the practice of "centralizing" masses and was condemned a second time in July 1875 by the authorities in Rome.

As with all that Migne did, it is difficult if not impossible, as we have seen so often, to determine with certainty whether his activities were essentially altruistic or self-serving, whether in this instance the application of his considerable entrepreneurial skills to the task of guaranteeing the performance of mass in dioceses lacking a priest constituted an act of efficient charity or one of self-interested simony. So too, it is hard to assess yet another area of Migne's economic activity alongside those of printing, the fabrication of religious objects, and the centralizing of masses—that is, the solicitation of loans from the lower clergy to whom he also hoped to sell the patrologies and the intricate calculation of interest on the money so obtained. At worst Migne joined the sin of usury to that of simony; at best, he charitably harnessed his considerable organizational capacities to the present needs of mid-century Catholicism under siege.

Les Prêtres Prêteurs

IN PROTECTING HIMSELF against Migne's unfortunate habit of appropriating that which he borrowed, Jean-Baptiste Malou (see above, p. 65) required a deposit for the loan of his copy of Rufinus ("mon Ruffin" [sic]); for, the cautious editor insists, "I believe that the man's interest in money is greater than memories or promises even." By "interest" Malou meant, of course, "economic motivation." But he could easily also have meant "interest" in the most literal sense of the term, for among all of Migne's myriad publicity and purchase schemes lies a simple interest in interest. We saw earlier the extent to which Migne's elaborate price schemes and payment schedules for the patrologies—the figures for pre-payment, payment upon delivery, and payment by installments—were determined by the precise calculations of the sums such money, if invested, might earn over time. Indeed, he is explicit about this consideration in announcing price reductions ("A Great Bonus in Advance Sale"): "This great bonus is due to his devotion to his work, his faith as an editor, finally to the interest he would draw on his funds if he invested them elsewhere" (AN F18 369).

Migne saw purchase of the patrologies as an investment, a placement of funds in the Ateliers catholiques, payment in advance simply being a means of lending cash for the purpose of furthering his good works. However, should the priest have the good fortune to have any fortune remaining after such a prepayment, and, pre-sumably, after purchasing any necessary accessories from Migne's "museum" of religious art, he would do well to make an outright loan. "Every time that we have had need of funds for a great undertaking, we have naturally turned toward our brothers in the

Priesthood and toward a few enlightened, pious, and comfortable laymen," Migne maintains in one of the prospectus appeals under the title of "A Licit, Advantageous, Dependable, Easy, and Worthy Means OF PLACING YOUR FUNDS." "Well, Providence has never permitted, not even once, that our appeal rest in vain. A new need presents itself today, that of pursuing with an unparalleled energy our previous and present publications."[34] Thus the complicated conditions under which the simple country priest might buy the *Cours complets* are mixed with the outright solicitation of loans, which become, under the Mignian rhetoric which endows the act of borrowing with grace, a deeply pious obligation. Nor, again, as we have seen with respect to Migne's journalism and activities as a publicist, did he invent anything new in allying the print industry with what amounted to a private bank. In the final section of Balzac's *Illusions perdues,* we find that the printing rivals of the hero David Séchard, the Cointet frères of Angoulême, have also unofficially entered the banking business, which gives them even greater facility in the financial ruin of all competition: "The firm of Métivier and the Cointet firm combined the function of bankers with their business as commission agents in paper supply, paper-manufacture and printing: be it said they were careful not to pay any licence for their banking activities. Taxation authorities have not yet found a way to keep such close surveillance on trading concerns as would enable them to force all those who carry on banking surreptitiously to take out a banking licence, which, in Paris for example, costs five hundred francs a year."[35]

Where Migne is concerned, all the historic arguments invoked by the Church against usury—that money is not a commodity to be bought and sold; that money, being sterile, cannot beget money; that to sell the same object at different moments for different prices is to sell time, which belongs only to God—are turned upon their head by Migne, who, in applying the work ethic to all that he did, could not tolerate the idea of money standing idle. He was haunted, in fact, by the notion of priests hoarding money in drawers throughout the countryside when he could put their savings to good use. And in encouraging full prepayment for the *Cours complets* rather than payment by quarterly installments, he reminds the potential subscriber of the horrors of sterile cash:

The editors only resort to this single draft, which, furthermore, is favorable to subscribers, whose funds would otherwise sleep sterilely in a corner of their desk, because of the infinite inconveniences and the considerable costs to them of four different drafts withdrawn at four different times. (AN F18 1803)

Migne, as we know, claimed to live like a monk, to abstain entirely from recreation ("not even one day in a lifetime"), to eat abstemiously, and, above all, to sleep very little. He was obsessed, in fact, by the idea of sleep, which implies a sinful barrenness subsumed in the abhorrent idea of "money sleeping sterilely in a corner of their [a priest's] desk"; and he promised his subscribers that he would not rest until the *Cours complets* had been completed: "If one asks us why we proceed so quickly, we will respond naively that it is in order to put our Fellow priests as well as right-thinking laymen in a position to profit sooner from a *Cours complet on each branch of Science;* and then in order to be able ourselves to collect ourselves a bit, after thirty years of an extraordinary extension of our intellectual and physical faculties."[36]

The metaphor of unproductive, sleeping funds obsessed Migne, who offered in the prospectuses to make the priest's sleeping money work for him: "It is thus at once a useful and worthy act, for those whose funds sleep unproductively, to consecrate them for a while to the increasingly rapid printing of the *Bibliothèque universelle du clergé.*" The lender who made available sleeping funds might himself sleep, since Migne would presumably work to make his money work while he—the priest—dozed: "After this act of high religious devotion and of enlightened prudence, these friends of the Church will be able to give themselves over to a saintly joy; for time running its precipitous course will bring them, even while they sleep, a material and spiritual good which contributes to their well being and to their glory."[37]

Among the many advantages which Migne extended to the priests who lent him money, only the first was that of sound sleep—the promise of a good night's rest: "Each lender will be able to sleep on both ears, without worrying in the least about the fate of his savings."[38] The other advantages seem to be modeled upon those which accrue to purchasers of both *Cours complets,* and which comes increasingly to resemble a sales formula applicable to all that Migne sold: 1) Free postage ("The cost of correspondence, sending and returning, will fall only upon us"); 2) Free pick-up ("We will collect, at our own expense, the funds from the residence of the priests"); 3) The choice of direct cash payment of interest due or an increased rate of return for payment in kind, that is to say, in books ("We will pay interest at the rate of 5% in cash, or 7% in bound volumes of their choice from among our publications");[39] 4) Liquidity of funds ("When they wish to withdraw their money, they will only have to notify us two months in advance"); 5) Regular dividends at borrower's expense ("As for interest payments, without [the lender's] even needing to request them, they will be sent every year, either in the form of bank notes or in postal vouchers purchased at our expense"). Finally, the most important inducement is that of honesty ("Thus, our priests will never see their rent clipped for any reason whatsoever").

Migne insists repeatedly upon the safety of funds lent to the Ateliers catholiques. The priests who place their funds with him can rest assured, first of all, because of Migne's reputation and his word:

You have known us for many years now where the greatest printing undertakings are concerned: you cannot forget who we are, known for our endowments as well as our publications: then, you probably respect us enough to be convinced that we would not accept funds so painfully amassed and so necessary perhaps to your old age if we believed them to be exposed to even the remotest risk. Well! We give you our word that all that you confide to us will be scrupulously returned, principal and interest.[40]

Lenders might also be reassured because of Migne's spotless record. His creditors, he asserts, have never lost a sou. Not during twenty-nine years of commercial dealings, not even during the financial crises following "the republican explosion," was a single bank note contested, a claim that is hard to believe, and even harder to believe that Migne believed, given the protracted disputes over the ownership of his newspaper empire (above pp. 26–32).[41] Be that as it may, those who will sleep better knowing their funds are safely invested need fear neither violence nor nocturnal pollution in their slumber: Migne's signature remains virgin— "*notre signature est restée vierge.*"

If Migne has never defaulted, it is also in part, he maintains, because of the cautious rate of return he offers. By paying no more than 5 percent he avoids unnecessary financial risk, as well as the potential moral risk of usury.[42] Besides, he reminds the reader and prospective lender, his rates are neither higher nor lower than those officially established by the Pope: "Our Holy Father the Pope has just offered a great example of Catholic conduct in this regard by giving out the shares of his borrowings at par and in only offering 5 percent annual revenue, in spite of the most critical circumstances and still more the funds having been alienated. In lending or in borrowing at the rate of the Sovereign Pontiff neither party needs to be ashamed or to make any kind of restitution: while who would dare let it be known that he has shamefacedly encouraged certain rates of interest commonly offered and accepted!" A deal is never quite a deal with Migne, however; and where money is concerned, the conditions of either purchase or loan seem, as we have seen with respect to the patrologies and the reimbursement for masses, to be almost infinitely flexible. The lender still not satisfied with the Pope's interest rate might, Migne allows, because of the financial solidity of the Ateliers catholiques, legitimately lend funds at a full percentage point higher than the official, morally sanctioned 5 percent, and the same holds true for alternate payment in books: "In spite of all that has been said up until now, if some Readers need for their funds to produce a slightly higher rate, we are happy to be able to say that our commercial strength allows us to offer them legally either 6% in cash, or 8% in volumes from among our publications."[43]

Further guarantee of the security of the funds lent to Migne lies in the simple fact that the value of his assets surpasses that of his debts ("Again, the warehouses are something so prodigious that even if they were sold for their paper contents to the grocer, and the same with the plates sold for their lead contents to the dealer in metals, the sum raised would greatly surpass our Liabilities"). Migne's enterprise is owned, he boasts, mortgage-free ("Add to that Monies Owed, the Newspaper, the Supplies, Furniture,

Museums, Libraries, Buildings and Land that appear immense to the eyes of all, and that we declare to be free of all mortgage").

Finally, if by some chance, disaster should befall either Migne or his operation, both are covered by a score of insurance companies whose names are printed—like the frontispiece to one of the volumes of the patrologies—by the entrance to the Ateliers catholiques:

In effect, in no imaginable circumstance, not even that of a fire, of the most extreme revolution or our death, would their funds be exposed to risk. And here are the reasons for such security: first, everything is insured by twenty Insurance Companies, whose plaques appear on the entrance [frontispice] of the building.[44]

Eternally optimistic, convinced of his own divine mission, a doer rather than a thinker, excessive in all he did, a brillant publicist for himself, Migne, as we shall see, could not have been more perversely prophetic.

The very names of the companies which had underwritten policies on the Ateliers catholiques inspired trust. Indeed, who could resist placing his or her money with, among others, la Paternelle, la Fraternelle, le Monde (the World), le Soleil (the Sun), l'Aigle (the Eagle), la France, la Clémentine, and la Confiance (Confidence)? The enterprise, backed by Migne's record of phenomenal accomplishment and extreme financial frugality, gave the impression of indisputable solidity.

With the patrologies almost completed, Bonnetty joins one last judgment to Migne's vaunt of invulnerability posted as a sign by the door. "Here they are at last finished, these two Patrologies, *Patrologie latine* and *Patrologie grecque,* the two most beautiful historical monuments to be found anywhere in the world!" he wrote in the *Annales de philosophie chrétienne* of 1866. "The Church only lives, only exists through its historical Traditions, only because it [tradition] proves that it [the Church] has existed since the beginning of time." The complete *Cours complets* offer living proof of the triumph of tradition, history, and theology over philosophy:

In vain does Philosophy, the heir to these Revelations, pretend at present to derive dogma and morality from itself, or accord itself the right to derive them directly from the Creator; if this school, which is arbitrarily called *independent philosophy* or *Catholic ontology*, were to become generally accepted, it would slowly displace even the idea of historical Revelations which God has shown to men, and which the Church merely preserves. . . . Given that one cannot derive the Revelations of God from oneself, or directly from the Creator, it is necessary to have recourse to historical Tradition which makes the Revelations known, that is to say to historical works of the authors which have kept for us the Traditions of the Church. Thus, it is precisely in the two precious collections of the *Patrologies* of M. l'abbé Migne that one finds, arranged according to chronological order, all the monuments of these ancient Traditions.[45]

The patrologies insure, as Migne had originally maintained, the perpetuity of the Church by making of its thought a monument inscribed not in stone but in metal, such a process of monumentalization constituting holy "titles of nobility," set—and the comparison could hardly be more apparent—against the devastating potential of the Revolution:

We have sometimes asked ourselves what will happen to such a collection of *plates*. If an *Ecclesiastical Assembly* still existed, we would ask it to acquire them. They are its titles of origin, of ownership and of nobility [*ses titres d'origine, de propriété et de noblesse*]; they belong to it and it cannot let them perish, especially at the very moment when, by means of these *plates*, these titles have become monuments etched, if not in stone, at least in metal, and as a result, are henceforth indestructible.[46]

The metal of the *plate*—the stereotype *cliché*—as a means of preserving Catholic writings in an age of mechanical reproduction becomes an arm for the waging of the contemporary battles of Christian history. It serves as a protective armor plate for the tradition rendered, in the Migne/Bonnetty martyrological rhetoric, "henceforth indestructible."

Trial by Fire

IT MUST HAVE come as some surprise, then, when the abbé Migne, his sleep in reality guaranteed by eighteen insurance companies, was awakened between one and two o'clock on the morning of February 12, 1868, to the news that the Ateliers catholiques were in flames, the fire having started somewhere in the print shop or between the print shop and the typesetters' room. Migne's first thought apparently was of his personal library. He began throwing books out of the window of his apartment before neighbors arrived to help save the furniture. The devastating fire, not contained until dawn, still smoldered in the morning. The journalists who arrived around seven observed that "the heat of the ground was still such that if paper fell upon it, it burst immediately into flame."[47] They seemed most impressed, however, by the images of melted metal, Bonnetty/Migne's arms and armor of Christian tradition, fused into bizarre blocks, liquefied into rivers, twisted and reduced to the brute state of raw material. "Five hundred thousand plates, stacked in piles, melted in an instant; they are now enormous blocks, in the most bizarre forms," we read in *Le Monde illustré*. "Thousands of volumes projected a flame which melted the plates, which were soon converted into a river of molten metal. . . . When day came, this immense workshop . . . was no more than a pile of blackened papers, of twisted steel in the midst of which enormous lead lingots could still be seen," echoes *Le Moniteur de Cantal*.[48] The final tally of Migne's metallic loss included 627,855 plates (*clichés*) and 582,722 kilos of lead, not counting an enormous organ, worth 30,000 francs and ready for delivery, which had melted so completely that, according to Alfred d'Aunay of *Le Figaro*, no trace remained.[49]

Migne showed remarkable fortitude and generosity immediately following the disaster. Though all that was left of the Ateliers catholiques were his own apartments and the accounts office, his second thought seems to have been directed toward the interests of those who had lent him money for interest: "My accounts office is intact. No one will lose anything [*Ma comptabilité est intacte. Personne ne perdra rien*]," he told *Le Figaro*.[50] The correspondent for the *Chronique du journal général de l'imprimerie* was impressed by the fact that "M. l'abbé Migne . . . has seen his steadfast work of thirty-five years perish in a few hours! Nonetheless, he is not discouraged." "I am very old, and I will finish my life's work before being myself finished," Migne is reported to have said.[51]

Bonnetty, who might even have known that one of the insurance companies whose name figured on the door of the Ateliers catholiques was the Phénix, paints a portrait of Migne rising from the ashes:

. . . a pile of smoking ruins, an inchoate mass of beams, of coals, of paper, of lead, all melted together . . . and then in a dark corner of this vast establishment, the irrepressible Migne, devastated, and saying these words to a friend who sought to console him: *They are no more!* Devastated, we say, but not beaten, still on his two feet and ready to recuperate, as much as it will be possible, from this immense disaster that would have been absolutely irreparable for anyone but him.[52]

Bonnetty, who had as early as 1861 placed Migne's colossal accomplishments within the realm of triumph over sinister prophecy ("thus as a result, all cynical prophecies concerning the impossibility of one man's accomplishing such a giant task are brought low"), Bonnetty, who just two years earlier had pronounced Migne's metallic monuments "henceforth indestructible," asks in an article entitled "Destruction of the Plates of All the Works of the Latin and Greek Fathers in a Fire at the Ateliers Catholiques of M. l'abbé Migne," "how the good Lord could have permitted such a disaster?" One can now, in the context of the earlier prideful boasts, detect a fulfillment of divine prophecy:

They are no more! . . . We have heard these painful words issue from the mouth of the indefatigable and matchless Editor of all the works of the Greek and Latin Fathers. In these immense workshops where, under the eye of the master, this army of workers worked . . ., reproducing the masterpieces of the human spirit, these traditions of the Catholic Church, . . . these titles of the beliefs and of the faith of our fathers, we have seen, one can say, the *Abomination of the desolation* of which the prophet speaks.[53]

The origin of the fire at the Ateliers catholiques, however suspicious, remains unknown. A letter of M. de Font-Réaulx written in 1875 affirms that l'abbé Ulysse Chevalier related that Migne considered it to have been set by a disgruntled worker; the concierges of the quarter spoke of a "fire set on purpose"—an *incendie volontaire*.[54] Both reports are on the order of hearsay, and the second is especially unworthy of belief, given the fact that Migne's insurance, as things turned out, and he could hardly have been unaware of the fact, was not all it was cracked up to be.

The popular weekly *L'Illustration* reported in the aftermath of the fire that: "One figure says it all. The abbé Migne estimates his losses to be twelve million, and the thirty-three companies [sic] whose names one used to see at the entrance to his establishment have only insured his creditors for six million" (February 22, 1868). The twenty companies that figured in Migne's pre-fire publicity were really only eighteen. In addition, Migne was covered for only twenty-nine fortieths of the worth of his assets, being self-insured for the remaining eleven-fortieths. If, as indicated above, Migne assured those who lent him money that "each lender will be able to sleep on both ears, without worrying in the least about the fate of his savings," now the lender could hardly rest easy on one ear. For the eighteen companies were not anxious to cover even the twenty-nine fortieths, and the protracted negotiations over reimbursement of Migne's losses were further delayed by the Franco-Prussian War and by the events of the Commune.

The case of the abbé Migne versus his insurers was finally heard in court only in December 1871.[55] And, like the police records which offer such a privileged glimpse into the everyday workings of the Ateliers catholiques, the transcript of the trial which appeared in the official legal journals not only sheds further light upon his finances, but also yields a fascinating account of what at the beginning of the Third Republic constituted the very nature and notion of a book.

The trial debate turned around the issue of the substance of Migne's loss, which was not as simple to assess as it might have seemed. The lawyers for the insurance companies tried to the extent possible to reduce the damage Migne had suffered. In the final hearing a M. Scellos, whose very name summons the idea of misdeed (Lat. *scelus*), emphasizes that:

1) the wear and tear of previous printings had reduced the value of the plates;

2) Migne's sales were diminishing, which means that the earning potential of the plates at the time of the loss no longer corresponded to their original earning power;[56]

3) some of the plates were worthless and others could be more

efficiently reproduced through movable type and not fixed clichés. Scellos includes in this category "almost all the Latin Patrology, with the exception of Saint Ambroise, Rufinus, Saint Jerome, Saint Augustine, Saint Leon, Saint Denis le Petit, Saint Gregory of Tours, Saint Bernard, the indexes, etc." as well as "a great part of the Greek Patrology";[57]

4) and, finally, Scellos argues that, according to law, an insurance policy should neither directly nor indirectly be the source of profit for the insured; to indemnify the abbé Migne for volumes that were selling poorly or not at all would be to allow him to amortize the payment over time. Migne, he argued, would simply print first the volumes which were selling best, leaving the others, for which he would also have been indemnified, until last.[58]

Migne was in some real sense hoisted by the petards of his own propensity for intricate and precise reckoning of sums due with interest over time. Indeed, the lawyers for the insurance companies proposed calculating the worth of Migne's publications volume by volume according to the number of copies printed, the number that survived, the number sold, and the rate of sales at the time of the fire. Scellos argues as follows where the *Dictionnaire de littérature,* for example, is concerned:

> . . . 1,050 copies of the Dictionary of Literature (2d series of the *Encyclopedia*) were printed in 1851; at the time of the fire 875 still remained; in eighteen years, he thus sold 175, or a little less than 10 per year. 375 copies were destroyed, which means that 510 [sic] survived the fire. Thus, assuming that annual sales were to continue at the same rate (which is a generous assumption), there would be enough copies in the warehouse to meet the sales demands of the next fifty-one years![59]

Migne met his match in his opponents who had, it seems, invented a scholastics of compensation worthy of his own outlandish calculations of labor, time, cost, and profit; nor were they, to judge by all that we have seen thus far, completely wrong to be suspicious of the consequences of such an enormous payment.

Migne's lawyers, on the other hand, sought to recuperate the entire cost of resetting in type the *Bibliothèque universelle du clergé.* The expert witness for the plaintiff, M. Firmin Didot of the publishing house which bears his name, emphasized:

1) The unique character of the loss ("the greatest publishing enterprise since the invention of printing").[60]

2) Its restitutive nature ("These objects are not exactly the same as, say, art objects, like paintings, statues, even jewels, since these 1,019 volumes could be reconstituted, page by page, line by line, by the Insurance Companies").

3) How close Migne was to completing the whole ("only several pages of the *Patrologies,* in 476 volumes, still remained to be printed").

4) The value of Migne's good works for Christianity ("M. Migne must thus be completely indemnified for the cost of the plates, or, and this would be an even greater solace for Christians, the plates should be reconstituted").

5) Finally, where the opposing experts on the question of "the estimated value of the industrial goods" had tried to separate the volumes of the *Bibliothèque universelle,* whose worth was calculated on an individual basis, Firmin Didot stressed the inseparability of the whole. The uniqueness of the collection resides in its completeness, no volume detachable from this "ensemble *sui generis*": "The separate parts which make up this whole depend upon and are linked to one another in such a way that even those which seem from a purely commercial point of view less valuable than others are nonetheless necessary to them."

In fact, Migne's actual material loss is extremely difficult to assess. The patrologies were within a hair's breadth of completion at the time of the catastrophe which befell him. The *Patrologie grecque* lacked but one volume, which had been set but not yet printed; and, as Bonnetty rightly remarked, "all would have been saved had the disaster occurred only two or three days later, since M. Migne only needs two days to print 1,000 copies of a volume."[61] Where the *Patrologie latine* was concerned, only the last three sheets of the last of six volumes containing the index remained to be completed.[62] Yet this represented no little undertaking: the first compilation of these tables took two years. So, we can assume that Migne, obsessed as he was by the idea of completion, had every intention of using at least part of such a lump sum indemnity to complete again the *Cours complets.* "As for M. Migne," affirms Bonnetty, quoting an interview with the abbé in the *Semaine reli-*

gieuse de Paris, "we know that in spite of the discouragement that such misfortune might have caused, he is resolved not to leave his life's work uncompleted. . . . He is going to begin work anew, redo the *tables of the Patrologie latine,* reset the melted plates of the *last volume of the Patrologie grecque* and of the other publications which we have mentioned."[63]

And yet, it is also reasonable to assume that Migne, who was seventy-one at the time of the settlement, could not possibly have reconstituted in their entirety the plates of the *Bibliothèque universelle du clergé.* "Without doubt he will not be able to completely raise from its ruins the edifice which has crumbled; but at least he wants to finish the works that were in the process of publication."[64] Nor is it out of the question to surmise, as his insurers must certainly have, that the industrious abbé, haunted by the idea of unproductive capital, money at rest, would have used that part of the settlement not required to restore and reset the tables for the *Patrologie latine* and the last volume of the *Patrologie grecque* for some other purpose, possibly even to earn interest. Indeed, such an assumption about lost time is in consonance with Firmin Didot's estimation of the compound nature of Migne's material loss: "It is necessary to compensate M. l'abbé Migne," his fellow editor claims, "for the delays which are detrimental to his commercial enterprise, delays which have already caused him such a great loss."

The case of Migne versus his insurers is significant in what it discloses about the nature of the book. The arguments on both sides are based upon radically different assumptions about the material worth of the printed page. For the lawyers for the eighteen insurance companies, the value of a book lies in the actual material worth that goes into its composition—that is to say, the paper and especially the metal of the plates: "582,722 kg. of lead from the type characters have been salvaged from the ruins." The companies propose to restitute only the commodity cost—"la valeur vénale"—of that which the fire destroyed, or a commercial value equivalent to fungibles like "wheat, flour, cotton, wool," to use the examples cited by Firmin Didot.[65]

For Firmin Didot the value of the book is assumed to be neither wholly material nor wholly immaterial. Unlike a fungible, the

Bibliothèque universelle projects an aura linked to its wholeness and its role—somewhat like a sacred relic—in Christian history. This makes it most like a jewel or a work of art, an object whose worth is determined by the surplus fetishized cultural value invested in it above and beyond the commercial worth of the material itself. And yet, the patrologies are unlike the unique piece of jewelry or art in that they are, Firmin Didot argues, replaceable through the labor of resetting them in type. Their worth inheres not in the magic of cultural fetishism, but in the investment in work they represent; and here it is hard to imagine a more labor-intensive investment, since the famous Tables, which lacked only three sheets at the time of the fire, capture, as Migne insists in the prepublication publicity, the very essence of concentrated toil, the equivalent of fifty thousand man-years of work distilled into three volumes—or, by implication, since only three sheets of the last tome remained to be done, into three pages. The formula devised by Firmin Didot for representing Migne's loss—the material object, physical and reproducible, yet nonetheless invested with something of the sacred—resembles nothing so much as the idea of the sacrament: the material object transformed into grace which, by a limitless economy of restituting that which allows reproduction, restores the independent volumes which are separate yet inseparable and whose collective essence is greater than the sum of their individual parts. Once again, for Migne private property is "the most sacred thing in the world after religion."

Nor could Firmin Didot's deposition have been more rhetorically effective. The third expert witness, a M. Daguin, called to decide between plaintiff and defendant, pronounced in favor of Migne, which resulted in the court ruling that:

1) The insurance companies must recognize formally that indemnity must correspond to cost of replacement;

2) The questions of which works have more or less "market value" and of what Migne would do with the money are irrelevant, since the advantage of receiving compensation in one lump sum would offset the loss in value of works currently out of circulation;

3) Where the question of the "plates and the industrial goods" is concerned, given that they were insured for 3,800,000 francs, that the adjusters' estimate is that before the fire they were worth

3,890,135 francs and 91 centimes, that the cost of clean-up was 340,457 fr. 05, the loss is set at 3,529,678 fr. 90.

Thus, "in applying the rule of proportionality and in deducting the eleven fortieths for which the abbé Migne was self-insured, the Companies owe 2,512,141 fr. 80." Migne received an additional 13,402 fr. 03 for the loss of buildings; 7,250 fr. for his private library; 411,699 fr. 95 for the books stored in the warehouses of the Ateliers catholiques; 224 fr. 74 for "the Stations of the Cross, paintings, organs and harmoniums"; 10,875 fr. for the big organ; 626 fr. 18 for his personal possessions. The court failed to sanction payment of interest on the money which remained dormant for the almost four years during which the Ateliers catholiques failed to print a single book. Migne, who eventually did reconstitute the famous Indices to the patrologies, lost his sight in the years between the fire and the settlement of his court case and, like some Balzacian character whose task had been completed, whose energy had been transferred into the object of his obsession, died in 1875.

❖   CONCLUSION

Le Bon Marché and the Ateliers Catholiques

Lost Illusions and the Printing Press

IF, IN LEARNING about Migne and the Ateliers catholiques of Montrouge, one often has the impression of reading a novel, or at least of having encountered the stuff of a novel, such an impression is not completely false; for there is almost no aspect of Migne's publicist or publishing activity that is not contained in Balzac's epic about the world of print culture under the Restoration, *Illusions perdues*. So thick, in fact, is the resemblance—the detailing of the techniques for producing and selling newspapers and books—that I found myself wondering more than once if Migne, before launching the *Bibliothèque universelle du clergé* in 1838, had read the first part of *Illusions perdues*, which appeared in February 1837. But since one can assume that Migne, who claimed not to have taken "even one hour of recreation a year," could hardly have had sufficient leisure to read a 700-page "grande petite histoire" ("big little tale"), as Balzac names the book, it seems unlikely that the ideas for his publishing and publicity schemes came directly from fiction. Besides, Migne's first journalistic dealings—the founding of the two newspapers *L'Univers religieux* and *Le Spectateur*, the shrewd dealings with Emmanuel Bailly, the aggressive absorption of the *Tribune catholique*—occurred in 1833 and could have served to inform Balzac of the machinations of the newspaper world just as well as did the other contemporaneous entrepreneurial hustlers and self-made men he encountered in the Paris of the 1820s and 1830s: César Birotteau of the *Courrier des spectacles,* Louis Reybaud of the *Constitutionnel,* or Ladvocat of the *Mercure de France.*

This is another way of saying that both Migne and Balzac were part of a moment of mighty change in the world of printing and

113

journalism, in the marketing of newspapers and books, and in the relation of both to a changing reading public. And if any conclusion is to be drawn from the fascinating story of the abbé Jacques-Paul Migne, it is one that seeks less merely to describe with wonder his extraordinary accomplishment than to situate it in the context of the immense shifts in the social and economic makeup of mid-century France. These, combined with significant advances in transportation and communication, allow us to see Migne as an embodiment of the industrial revolution of the Restoration and July Monarchy, and as a paradigm of the print capitalists captured with such an intense impression of historical accuracy in Balzac's fictional account. Migne may have possessed the focused energy of a Balzacian hero, but he was in some more deeply comprehensible way the pure product of the times Balzac chronicles in *La Comédie humaine*, right down to the techniques for book production and distribution. Indeed, now that we have seen *what* Migne did, it is clear that one answer to the question, posed at the outset, of *how* he did it is purely technical.

The Migne phenomenon would have been unthinkable without the enormous advances, first of all, in the manufacture of paper that is, on the level of theme, the subject of *Illusions perdues*. Balzac, through the character of David Séchard, is novelistically obsessed by the search for a low-cost paper to meet the very real expanding demands of book and newspaper publishing in the post-Revolutionary period. Supposedly set in 1822–23, *Illusions perdues* is suffused with the spirit of the increasing appetite of a growing reading public whose need for paper can no longer be met by the traditional means of paper manufacture from hemp and linen rag:

At present paper is still made with hemp and linen rags; but this ingredient is dear, and its dearness is holding back the great momentum which the French Press will inevitably acquire. . . . If therefore the needs of the paper industry become greater than France's supply of rags, two or three times greater, for instance, in order to keep paper cheap, it would be necessary to make it out of some other material than rags.[1]

The search for a vegetable substitute for rag which consumes David Séchard in the third section of *Illusions perdues*, "The Inventor's

Tribulations," reflects a historical problem of paper supply which was not resolved until 1846 by the fabrication of paper from a mixture of defibrated sawdust bonded chemically and not mechanically—the acidified paper whose disintegration is currently of such worry. And although truly cheaper paper appeared on the scene two years after the first volume of the patrologies, a number of lesser innovations in the techniques of manufacture did make Migne's ambition of rendering books accessible at the lowest possible cost more feasible in 1838 than it would have been only fifty years earlier.

Vellum paper, smoother and therefore more easily printable, began to replace the older wire-laid paper around the middle of the 1700s.[2] More important, not only did more efficient—that is, mechanical—means of paper production came into being in the last years of the eighteenth and the first quarter of the nineteenth century, but the very form of paper production shifted away from the single sheet toward the continuous roll. Louis Robert of the paper factories of Essonne had obtained a patent for a continuous paper machine in 1798, and the first prototype was working in England in 1803. The machines developed in France after 1814, enhanced by certain ameliorations in the actual process of mixing the paper *pâte,* were capable of producing one thousand kilograms of paper per day instead of the previous one hundred produced by hand.[3]

To the increased capacity of paper manufacture were added immense advancements in the efficiency of the printing press, which had changed very little, in fact, between the invention of printing and the first quarter of the nineteenth century. The fifty years following the democratic revolutions in America and France represent a period of keen progress in press design as well as in the systems of inking and typesetting. The wooden hand presses that had not changed much since the time of Gutenberg were gradually replaced by more dynamic metal machines. Wilhelm Haas of Basle had developed in the 1770s and 1780s a semi-metal two-stroke press with a stone chassis. A single-stroke version with double the power of the common screw press devised by the Didot family of Paris was apparently stolen by E. A. J. Anisson-Duperron, Directeur de l'Imprimerie Royale.

Philippe-Denis Pierres made a number of improvements—a platen double the size of that of preexisting presses, a cam movement instead of a screw, a vertical lever in the place of the horizontal bar. To these were added the "wheel press" of Benjamin Dearborn (1785), which permitted printing of a whole sheet with one pull of the lever, and the spring press of Thomas Prosser (1794), which allowed pressure on the platen to be regulated.[4] All of the late eighteenth-century improvements on the wooden hand press culminated, however, in the all-metal Stanhope press (1804), which was introduced to France by Ambroise Firmin Didot shortly after the Napoleonic wars and whose impact was such that Balzac uses it in the very first sentence of *Illusions perdues* to mark the difference not only between Paris and the provinces, but between the present moment of printing (1822) and the archaic, "groaning" past: "At the time when this story begins, the Stanhope press and inking-rollers were not yet in use in small provincial printing-offices. Angoulême, although its paper making industry kept it in contact with Parisian printing, was still using those wooden presses from which the now obsolete metaphor 'making the presses groan' originated."

The period between 1810 and the 1830s when Migne began printing was the formative period in the mechanization of printing. Alongside the Stanhope press stood Koenig and Bauer's cylinder machine, whose steam-driven platen marked a perceptible threshold in the mechanical era of print.[5] Though the first Koenig presses were manufactured in London (and later in Germany), they were quickly exported, as Cowper claimed in a speech before the Royal Institution (1828), "to the most celebrated printers of London, Paris, and Edinburgh."[6] By 1823 the Parisian *Bulletin des lois* had a two-cylinder machine manufactured by Applegath, who had improved Koenig's rollers; Firmin Didot used a "big cylinder press" alongside the Stanhope press he had purchased less than a decade earlier. Between 1828 and 1830 some twenty Koenig machines were sold in France, until Gaveaux's two-cylinder machine manufactured for *Le National* (1831) signaled the advent of the French versions of the Koenig, an entrance of the French press-makers upon the scene, which was capped in 1854 by Auguste Hippolyte Marinoni's four-feeder cylinder machine made for *La Presse*.[7]

With the increased efficiency of printing presses came other essential improvements in the area of inking and typesetting. Balzac's archaic press of *Illusions perdues,* for example, is one whose ink is still applied manually by means of leather balls: "Printing there was so much behind the times that the pressmen still used leather balls spread with ink to dab on the characters." Yet Cowper (1818) and Appelgath (1823) developed improved mechanical inking rollers for Koenig's press; Gannal and Les Mame of Paris, printers of religious books alongside Migne, began using gelatinous rollers made out of a combination of sugar and adhesive as early as 1819.[8] Balzac notes in his fictional but nonetheless accurate account of the history of printing under the Restoration that David Séchard, in taking over his father's presses just three years later (1822), immediately abandoned the old leather tampons in favor of new cylindrical ink rollers: "Three months after his arrival in Angoulême David had replaced the old-fashioned ink-balls with a table and rollers made of glue and molasses which gave a smooth and even distribution of ink."[9]

Improvements in presses and in inking were accompanied by some progress in solving the age-old difficulties of typesetting— that is, the problem of reordering disassembled type once printing had taken place and of storing pages set in print for books still available. Between 1797 and 1798 Herhan, Firmin Didot, and Gatteaux obtained a patent for a system of stereotyped plates which, through a cold striking of the mold in a block of metal, offered improved clarity. In 1855 Adrien Delcambre developed a pianotype typesetter, which probably arrived on the scene too late for Migne, who, it will be remembered, lost in the fire of 1868 some 582,722 kilos of lead characters and 627,855 stereotype plates.

It is difficult to tell whether the technological innovations in printing of the first third of the nineteenth century—the advent of continuous paper, of the metal Stanhope press and the mechanical steam-driven Koenig, of cylindrical inkers, and of improved typesetting—represent a response to, or an effect of, an increased demand for print in the post-Revolutionary period. Yet, of this there can be no doubt: such advances meant necessarily lower book prices, and lower prices in turn increased demand. Migne's ambition of making the maximum number of books available to the widest possible audience at the lowest price was, again, part of a larger trend.

The print industry grew phenomenally after the Consulate and during the Restoration. Between 1811 and 1840 the number of print shops increased by 150 percent or twice as fast as the population, such rapid growth ending only with the tighter surveillance of the press during the Second Empire, declining to 108 percent in the 1840s and to 98 percent in the 1850s. The rate of book publication, which is estimated to have been less than two thousand titles per year before the Revolution, grew, according to the *Bibliothèque de France,* to 2,547 titles in 1814, and to 8,237 titles in 1826; then, after a decline to 5,530 titles in 1847, it again increased to 12,269 titles in 1869. The number of Parisian booksellers grew from 310 in 1804 to 434 in 1826.[10] Moreover, if the Restoration was synonymous with an increase in the rate of publication, that expansion was, as things turn out, nowhere more pronounced than in the realm of religious editions. Despite the secularization of primary public education after the Guizot law of 1833 and of secondary education after 1840, the return of monarchy implied not only a Catholic "Restoration" (above, pp. 10–12), but, more specifically, an augmentation in the number of religious titles.

The impact of a closer relation between altar and throne upon the print industry did not escape the attention of Balzac, who is ever aware of the least barometric change in the marketing atmosphere. David Séchard's competitors, the Cointet, turn, like a cynical version of Migne, in this direction: "The brothers Cointet adopted the views of the monarchist party, made an open show of keeping fast-days, haunted the Cathedral, cultivated the society of priests and brought out reprints of books of devotion as soon as they came into demand. Thus they took the lead in a lucrative side-line."[11] In interpreting the above passage, we must bear in mind that this "demand" for religious books, fictionally situated in 1822, is itself rooted, like the contemporaneous castles in Renaissance paintings of the nativity, in the first part of a novel which appeared in 1837, or just a year before Migne launched the *Bibliothèque universelle du clergé.* Indeed, since the 1838 prospectus we examined at some length, as well as the letterhead on

Migne's stationery, alludes to "letters of consultation" dispatched the previous year, one is tempted to speculate that Migne, fresh from his journalistic experiences with *l'Univers* and *l'Univers religieux,* must have conceived the idea of an integral Catholic library in a time frame practically simultaneous with the appearance of *Illusions perdues.*

Migne not only sensed, like Balzac, the market for religious publications, but, and here we arrive at the more specific dimensions of his accomplishment, he capitalized upon the equally powerful contemporaneous current toward complete editions published in series. The Consulate and the Empire had witnessed the publication of several series of complete editions of classical works. During the Restoration this tendency toward *oeuvres complètes* forming "libraries" focused upon national literature, with, for example, the publication in 1816 by Théodore Desoer of a twelve-volume Voltaire in octavos, and with the appearance from Lèfevre, Cérioux, and Renouard of the complete works of Voltaire, Rousseau, and Montesquieu, as well as a 73-volume octavo edition from Lèfevre of French classics.[12] More important, however, these were marketed, like Diderot's Encyclopedia and Beaumarchais's edition of Voltaire, not individually, not as a whole to be purchased all at once in one lump sum, but sequentially and by subscription, a sales technique that is not unfamiliar to, in fact is the very essence of, Migne's marketing of the Church Fathers. What this means, again, is that the director of the Ateliers catholiques invented less than he assimilated the marketing trends of the time.

Shrinking National Space

IF MIGNE WAS the product of a particular moment in the history of printing and publication, to which he also contributed, that contribution would have been impossible without the industrial revolution which began in France in the 1840s. Any understanding of how he did as much as he did must begin from the assumption of a virtual revolution in the demographic, economic, and technological makeup of mid-century France. We have seen that Migne left the provinces as a result of disagreement with the ecclesiastical hierarchy. He was swept to the capital on a demographic tide that saw Paris grow from 547,000 inhabitants in 1800 to 1,000,000 in 1850. His arrival in Paris is, in fact, illustrative of my larger point about his status as both the agent and the object of contemporaneous trends: having followed the crowd from the periphery to the center, Migne then drew others to Montrouge.

The growth of the print industry, of which the fortunes of the Ateliers catholiques seem exemplary, was part and parcel of a greater economic takeoff, which also influenced markets in a way directly accountable for Migne's success once he had settled in Paris. The July Monarchy is synonymous with economic, industrial, and territorial expansion. France expanded, first, abroad; and the decision of 1840 to remain in Algeria signaled the beginning of a second colonial empire, which eventually surpassed the first. But France also experienced a period of unprecedented economic growth and transformation at home. As F. Crouzet, M. Lévy-Leboyer, and T.-J. Markovitch have shown, the middle decades of the century "reveal," in the phrase of David Pinkney, "an extraordinary phase of acceleration in industrial production."[13] Indeed, Crouzet demonstrates that beginning in 1841 industrial production, measured as a percentage of the average annual production between 1815 and 1913, shows an increase of 15 percent in 1841, growing steadily to 30 percent in 1846 and, after that (with the exception of the crisis years 1847–48), to a peak in 1853, and continuing at high levels throughout the 1850s and 1860s.[14] This meant increased marketing potential, though the demand for religious encyclopedias can hardly be considered to be as expansive as that for secular books, which profited during the first half of the century from the increased literacy of the general population. It also implied an expansion of the market which Migne saw specifically as his own. For, with the rapid growth of agricultural production between 1820 and 1870 one can only assume that the purchasing power of the rural clergy, the curés de campagne toward whom the patrologies were aimed, increased proportionally, as attested by Migne's appeals for investment of their surplus cash and by his horror of money lying unproductively throughout the countryside.[15]

The acceleration of production in the 1840s through the 1860s was enabled by immense technological advances which were, I think it can be shown, responsible not only for an industrial modernism that I have identified with the productive capacity of the Ateliers catholiques, but for a virtual revolution in the means of merchandising consumer goods, including books. Migne was, as we have seen, at the forefront of the application of steam-driven presses to the mission of Catholic renewal. In this too he was part of his time. The decades of mid-century are the decades of steam, the number of engines used in industry growing from approximately 150–200 in 1816 to 1,447 in 1835, to 2,591 in 1840, and to 4,900 in 1850. Between 1840 and 1860 the combined horsepower of industrial steam power increased from 37,000 to 166,000.[16] The steam-driven printing press embodied the principle of efficiency which Migne captures in the comparison of a single minute of the press's productivity to three years of manual labor on the part of a monk (above, p. 85). Then too, the mechanical efficiency of the steam engine, expressed through an image of compressed time, finds its spatial counterpart in the application of steam to the means of transportation which, along with improved means of communication, made France from the 1840s on seem like a smaller place.

The decisive phase of French railroads began with an 1842 law and the construction of a network of lines radiating from Paris. Before the 1840s there were less than 1,000 kilometers of track, in 1848 there were 1,830 kilometers, and by 1860 there were more than 8,000. The coming of rail lines, complemented by the tripling of canals between 1815 and 1848 and the development of roads under the July Monarchy, both increased the speed and lowered the cost of transporting goods by more than half in the first half of the century. Railroads and roads made the mail faster and more reliable. Combined with the establishment of the first telegraph line in the very year of the first volume of the patrology (1844), they increased the efficiency of communication in a way that had a direct effect on the nature and volume of commerce, and, more specifically, upon the means at Migne's disposal for the mass marketing of the Fathers.

Wholesale Drygoods and the Fathers of the Church

THE TREMENDOUS IMPROVEMENTS in transportation and communication of the 1840s through the 1860s, which were practically coterminous with the decades of the *Bibliothèque universelle du clergé* (1838–68), made new markets more readily accessible. And this accessibility enabled, indeed became almost synonymous with, a retail system based upon an economy of scale. The rapid movement of goods and information throughout France—by road, canal, rail; by telegraph and improved mail—was probably the single most important factor in creating the conditions under which the guild system of the Ancien Régime, predicated upon a maintenance of craftsmanship and the steady procurement of supplies as well as upon preventing unfair pricing and the encroachment of one small merchant upon another, was transformed into a system of merchandising by wholesale: that is, the purchase of supplies, often through third-party agents, at discount and in bulk, mass manufacture of standardized objects, and volume sales at the lowest possible price.

And Migne was about nothing, if not about **wholesale:** His goal, "to render Christian tradition accessible and intelligible to all," and his creed—"the good at a good price"—capture in another register, and in connection with a commodity which we do not customarily associate with commercialization, the mid-century trend toward a mass market, bureaucratization, and rationalization of economic exchange.

It would be worth knowing, and I must admit that the question has occurred more than once in the preparation of this little book, just where the abbé Jacques-Paul Migne, trained in the provinces in the ways of the Lord, might have learned so quickly the ways of the world. How did he assimilate so naturally, almost immediately upon arriving in Paris, the mass marketing techniques characteristic not only of the selling of the Fathers through the Ateliers catholiques, but of the publicity and pricing schemes that are the very essence of what was a virtual revolution in retail?

The answer resides partially in that zone where Migne's considerable personal energy, his Balzacian drive, intersects with the social, economic, and technological tenor of the times. Yet, it also lies in some profound sense in a literal understanding of Migne's own dictum, "du bon, à bon marché," steered in the direction of that other incarnation of the mass market—the Bon Marché, the department store whose innovative product line, publicity, and sales methods resonate uncannily with the very concept of and the modes of marketing of the *Cours complets*. The earliest of the *magasins de nouveauté* appeared, like Migne, in the Paris of the 1830s (Le Bon Marché, Petit Saint-Thomas). They multiplied throughout the 1840s (Ville de Paris), the 1850s (Louvre, Bazar de l'Hôtel de Ville), 1860s (Printemps), the 1870s (Samaritaine), and even the 1890s, with the creation of the Galeries Lafayette.[17] Both the sales techniques and the types of goods sold in the department store were far from the artisanal modes of the small specialty shops, and far from them in a way thoroughly analogous to the distance between Migne's thousand-volume *Bibliothèque universelle du clergé* and almost all previous efforts to edit the Church Fathers.

Where the small specialty shops offered primarily a single type of merchandise, the *grands magasins* sold a wide range of goods, and within each product category a full line. Where existing editions of the Fathers had been conceived according to individual authors or single genre or topic series, Migne sought to reproduce within a single frame the entire tradition. The notion of selling Christian tradition *in toto* was, as we have seen, essential. Migne also sold a diverse line of other services, from newspapers and books to religious art, to the procurement of masses and the return of interest on pious loans. The Ateliers catholiques was not simply a book shop, but contained as well a library, a bookstore, a chapel, a bindery, a foundry, a warehouse, an artist's atelier, a "museum," and a bank.

Where the small specialty shops practiced only minimal advertising, consisting primarily of street cries or signs, the department store developed an elaborate system of almanacs, prospectuses, and catalogues, the first of which was proffered from the Petit Saint-Thomas in 1844, the year, again, of the first volume of the patrologies, and refers specifically to discount prices, a recently organized mail-order service, and special sales.[18] Migne was, as we have seen, the "Napoleon of the prospectus," whose special pricing offers and subscriptions by mail, for the purpose of selling the writings of the Saints, among whom Saint Thomas, are in keeping with both the spirit and the marketing techniques of the Petit Saint-Thomas. We have also noted that both Migne and the directors of the Bon Marché placed similar paid newspaper articles of their own design in the supposedly independent popular press.

More important, in the place of the primarily handmade goods of the specialty shops, the department store sold mass-produced standard items at the lowest fixed price, such standardization also lying at the heart of Migne's conception of the *Cours complets*. Migne envisioned the *Bibliothèque universelle du clergé* in mass terms, as attested to not only by the five thousand letters of consultation dispatched throughout the world and the fifty thousand letters of praise supposedly received in return, but in the very proposition of abundant sales by mail which assumes a potential market extending to the whole of France and beyond. The tension, in fact, between the Ateliers catholiques and the small retail booksellers of Paris (above, pp. 91–92), which in many ways is comparable to the struggle between the small specialty shops and the *grands magasins,* stems precisely from the difference between traditional-minded merchants content with a predictable local clientele and the impersonal wholesaler whose market is conceived to be as large as the globe.[19] The publications of the Ateliers catholiques are, Migne maintains repeatedly in the prospectuses, not only economical, but they are also uniform, each volume, each page, and each column resembling every other, consistency being the guarantee of quality. Similarly, if the *grands magasins* could be said to have any particular forte, any long suit, it was from the beginning the standard garment, the ready-made suit, as opposed to the tailor-made clothing of the smaller shops or even the secondhand clothing shop that figures so crucially in the middle section of *Illusions perdues.*

And here we have it: the answer to the questions of how Migne could have printed as much as he did and how he could have known as much about marketing what he printed is, simply put, **drygoods.** The *magasins de nouveautés* grew out of drygood or drapery stores selling cloth, clothing, haberdashery, lingerie, furs, napery, sewing notions, and other fancy goods, the very word "nouveauté" being synonymous with items in and around the textile trade.[20] Migne too came from drygoods, the Maison Delcros-Migne of Saint-Flour, with which he remained in regular contact while in Paris, from whom he received financial assistance in addition to all his clothing and table linen, and to whom he dispatched volumes of the *Cours complets* for sale in his native Auvergne.

To say that the key to understanding Migne's prodigious productive capacity lies in *wholesale* and in *drygoods* is certainly not to imply that Migne received specific marketing ideas from home, since it seems improbable that even a prosperous provincial drapery store would be in advance or even comparable to the *grands magasins* of Paris where merchandising is concerned. Nor does it seem likely that Migne rushed, upon arrival in the capital, to study the *magasins de nouveautés,* which were in the 1830s not as forward-looking in their sales techniques as was the 1838 prospectus of the Ateliers catholiques.[21]

What does seem probable, first, is that Migne learned many of the techniques of producing and marketing the Church Fathers, techniques that would become the *modus operandi* of the Ateliers catholiques, from the world of newspaper journalism and editing that he encountered upon arrival in Paris, techniques that were, moreover, clearly common practice, as we see in *Illusions perdues:* the technology of mechanical printing, the buying and selling of two newspapers for the price of one, the principle of mass circulation at low prices, the practice of the "reprint digest" transformed into the reprinting of previously published material not in the public domain, the circulation of prospectuses or broadsheets as a means of advertising, the placement of self-generated favorable reviews in the mouths of others.

What this suggests, second, is that both the Migne phenomenon and that of the *magasins de nouveautés* were ripe for the wholesale commodification of books and drygoods that followed upon the acceleration of transportation and communication which provided such a fertile network for mass commerce. If Migne and the *grands magasins* operated according to the principles and practices of bulk purchase, standardization, high turnover, appeal to a global market, rationalization of low fixed prices, mail order, prospectuses, and catalogues, etc., it is because such techniques of manufacture and marketing—that is to say, of wholesale mass production and distribution—must have appeared as the syllogistic conclusion to the logic of demographic, economic, and technological takeoff of mid-century, or to the sense of accelerating time and shrinking national space within a world, not unlike that of our own information revolution, made faster and smaller by technological progress.

The technology of the 1840s is, in the final analysis, the referent for Migne's own vision of the thoroughly modern industrio-spiritual project of the mass production and marketing of the Church Fathers. He imagines, as we have seen, the effect of his publications in terms of a constriction of space; he represents himself as a trail blazer, an explorer who has found in the *Cours complets,* particularly in the Indices of the patrologies, a shortcut to mastering Christian tradition: "Thanks to our Tables, these great series are rendered small; distances are closer together, the first and the last volumes touch" (*PL* 218, col. 4). Migne literally compares his publications to the tunnel blasted through Mount Cenis, through which he will drive the train of the Fathers. Which means, again, that the *Bibiothèque universelle du clergé* can be most appropriately understood in the context of the contemporaneous manufacturing and technological takeoff of which it is an exemplary part—the shortening of time through the use of mechanical energy and the shrinking of space through roads, the railroad, and the telegraph. In no other way, finally, can we assimilate Migne's analogy of the publication of the Church Fathers to electricity and flight—"What an economy of time! It's better than the railroad, and even the balloon, it's electricity!" (*PL* 218, col. 4).

To end by repeating Migne's hymn to technology is not to suggest the primacy of the technical or the triumph of rationalistic means of production over the spiritual; rather, to suggest that the project of mass production and marketing characteristic of both the rise of the department store and the Ateliers catholiques became, in the last half of the nineteenth century and in the first part of our own, not only a form of religion in its own right, but a particular quality of modernism itself. The department store of the Third Republic was, like the Ateliers catholiques, which conceived itself along the lines of the monastery, an "internal work community," a House, whose institutionalized paternalism replaced traditional family relations within, in the words of Michael Miller, "an impersonal and rationalized work environment."[22] For the potential shopper it represents, as Zola maintains through the repeated religious metaphors of his department store novel, *Au*

Bonheur des dames, a "commercial cathedral" right down to the airy—that is, gothic—steel and glass construction of the modernist style of the Belle Epoque: "One gained space everywhere, air and light entered freely, the public circulated easily, under the solid thrust of a long framework of beams. It was a cathedral of modern commerce, solid and light, made for a people of clients."[23] Aristide Boucicaut of the Bon Marché offered a guided tour of the House each day at 3 P.M. Migne, some decades earlier, encouraged similar visits with an invitation printed on top of the stationery of the Ateliers catholiques as well as in the prospectus "Curieux détails" (see above, p. 54). Both conceived of the enterprise at whose head they stood as, respectively, a commercial and an industrial shrine to which pilgrimage was encouraged.

Finally, Migne's comparison of the patrologies to the railroad, electricity, and the balloon anticipates nothing so much as the prime metaphor of the birth certificate of modern poetry, Guillaume Apollinaire's "Zone":

> Only religion is still new only religion
> Has stayed simple like the Airport hangars
>
> In all Europe you alone are not antique O Christianity
> The most up-to-date European is you Pope Pius X

Apollinaire, who published his own *bibliothèques complètes* of pornography rather than of the Church Fathers, nonetheless seized something fundamental which Migne had had a hand in creating—the transformation of the press into a religion revealed in the advertising apparitions of the prospectus, the catalogue, the newspaper, and the *affiche:*

> And you whom the windows stare at shame keeps you back
> From going into some church and confessing your sin
>   this morning
> You read the prospectuses the catalogues the public
>   notices that sing out
> Here's the morning's poetry and for prose we have
>   newspapers

This is not to suggest, again, that Migne advocated, or even understood, the poetic modernism which "Zone" captures. Yet the implications of the technological revolution of mid-century, of which he was aware and which determined his own vision of himself, engendered nonetheless a shrinking sense of time and space whose omnipresent simultaneous perceptual potential will culminate around the turn of this century in, among other things, cubism and vorticism in painting and sculpture, in scientific theories of relativity and uncertainty, in historicism, in the contextualizing interpretive impulse of psychoanalytic theory, and even in the involuntary memory of a Marcel Proust, for whom the redefinition of relations of time and space—the commingling of communication and communion—becomes a new religion of art. For the abbé Jacques-Paul Migne it is, again, by publishing Tertullian, the first of the Church Fathers, that the future will become manifest: "In this world anxious for Progress, we offer the Tradition of the past in order to march forward. *Traditio tibi praetendetur auctrix* (Tert., *de Coron. milit.*, cap. 4)."

❖ NOTES

Chapter 1

1. For a more complete and detailed description of Migne's corpus see L. Marchal's article on Migne in the *Dictionnaire de théologie catholique,* 10.2, col. 1728–38.

2. Archives nationales F18 333a (June 28, 1854), hereafter referred to as AN; see also Pierrard, Pierre, "L'Abbé Migne journaliste" in *Migne et le renouveau des études patristiques. Actes du colloque de Saint-Flour, 7-8 juillet, 1975,* eds. Mandouze, André, and Fouilheron, Joël (Paris: Beauchesne, 1985), p. 110.

3. "Il est bien bon que le lecteur le sache, nous ne prenons pas une heure de recréation par an" (cited Hamman, A.-G., *Jacques-Paul Migne. Le retour aux Pères de l'Eglise* [Paris: Beauchesne, 1975], pp. 73). The comparison did not escape contemporaries. The newspaper *Le Droit* of December 22, 1871, speaks of Migne's publishing enterprise as "the most colossal of this century, an undertaking that recalls the patient work of the monks of the middle ages."

4. Cited Hamman, *Migne,* pp. 73–74.

5. *Annales de philosophie chrétienne,* 3e série, vol. 14 (1846), p. 394.

6. Cited Soltner, Louis, "Migne, Dom Guéranger et Dom Pitra" in *Colloque de Saint-Flour,* p. 205.

7. "I beg you to inform me if since your visit of last May 23rd, the Ministry of Religious Affairs (*le ministère des cultes*) has discovered the new residence of M. l'abbé Romaine, vicar of St. Louis of Oran, then curé of Bougie, a post that he left after his dismissal. Mgr the Bishop of Alger had allowed him to move about freely where he wanted, and he is believed to have made it to California. He owes me 190 for 30 volumes of the Cours des Orateurs. I would be much obliged, Monsieur le ministre, if you would inform me whether or not he is collecting any kind of state pension" (AN F19 5842).

8. Letter to Dom Pitra of January 22, 1965, cited in Hamman, *Migne,* p. 84.

9. *Annales de philosophie chrétienne,* 5e série, t. 10, vol. 69 (1864), pp. 81, 83. The comparison with Hercules is repeated in col. 1, vol. 218,

of the *PL:* "Après tout cela, n'avons-nous pas le droit de nous écrier: Que sont les douze Travaux d'Hercule auprès de nos 231 Tables!"

10. Marchal, "Migne," col. 1723.

11. *La Littérature religieuse d'avant-hier et d'aujourd'hui* (Paris, 1906), p. 19. Cited in Hamman, *Migne,* p. 151.

12. "This work should be protected more than it is by the government, by the bishops, and by all Catholics. We must come to the assistance of this tireless and courageous editor. For we know that at the present moment he does not have yet enough subscribers to cover his printing costs. And what's more, most of his subscribers are foreigners, Protestants or Greeks" (*Annales de philosophie chrétienne,* 4e série, vol. 47 [1853], p. 162).

13. *Annales de philosophie chrétienne,* 5e série, t. 10, vol. 69 (1864), p. 84.

14. *Annales de philosophie chrétienne,* 5e série, t. 14 (1866), pp. 412–13. See also Vernet, André, "L'abbé Jacques-Paul Migne (1800–75) et les ateliers du Petit-Montrouge," *Annuaire de la Société Historique du 14e Arrondissement* (1960), p. 40.

15. Barbier, Hippolyte, *Biographie du clergé contemporain par un solitaire* (Paris: A. Appert, 1841), pp. 304–5.

16. Barbier, *Biographie,* p. 306.

17. Hamman, *Migne,* p. 55.

18. Cited Hamman, *Migne,* p. 84.

19. Cited Hamman, *Migne,* p. 124.

20. Letter of February 25, 1842, cited in Hamman, *Migne,* p. 116.

21. Letter of February 13, 1858, Bibliothèque nationale (hereafter referred to as BN), n. a. 24633, fol. 478.

22. Cholvy, Gérard, and Hilaire, Yves-Marie, *Histoire religieuse de la France contemporaine* (Paris: Privat, 1985), 13–20.

23. See Pinkney, David H., *Decisive Years in France. 1840–47* (Princeton: Princeton University Press, 1986), pp. 68–79.

24. See Leflon, Jean, "Crise et Restauration des foyers de science religieuse dans l'église du XIXe siècle," in *Colloque de Saint-Flour,* pp. 53–59; Cholvy, Gérard, "La Restauration catholique en France au XIXe siècle" (1801–1860), in *Colloque de Saint-Flour,* pp. 61–89; Cholvy and Hilaire, *Histoire religieuse,* pp. 20–39.

25. Hamman, *Migne,* p. 76. He is perceived even by contemporaries as having done just that. In one of the rare moments of official recognition Migne was praised on the floor of the Senate by a perhaps not completely impartial witness of the Revolution, M. le Baron Charles Dupin, for "the

reparation of a great devastation" (*Annales de philosophie chrétienne,* 5e série, t. 6, vol. 65 [1862], p. 244).

26. Prospectus of Migne reproduced in F. Mély, "L'abbé Migne. L'homme et l'oeuvre," *Revue archéologique* 5 (1915): p. 227.

27. Letter of July 8, 1838 (AN F18 1803). See Savart, Claude, "Un editeur révolutionnaire au service de la tradition," in *Colloque de Saint-Flour,* p. 146.

28. "Solesmes éditera le *Cours de Patrologie,* aura la direction exclusive de l'oeuvre quant à la révision doctrinale et typographique de la copie et devra se charger des tables. Cadence de livraison: trois volumes par mois. Rémuneration: 200 fr. par volume." (Soltner, Louis, "Migne, Dom Guéranger et Dom Pitra. La collaboration solesmienne aux entreprises de Migne," in *Colloque de Saint-Flour,* pp. 199–200).

29. Soltner, in *Colloque de Saint-Flour,* p. 202.

30. Soltner, in *Colloque de Saint-Flour,* p. 195.

31. "In another age," writes the abbé Brémond in 1906, "one can easily imagine a monument [to Migne] placed opposite that of Balzac" (cited in Hamman, *Migne,* p. 152).

32. See Hamman, *Migne,* pp. 63–64.

33. Barbier, Frédéric, "L'Industrialisation des techniques," in *Histoire de l'édition française,* ed. Martin, Henri-Jean, and Chartier, Roger (Paris: Promodis, 1985), t. 3, "Le Temps des éditeurs du Romantisme à la Belle Epoque," p. 72.

34. Collingham, H. A. C., *The July Monarchy* (London: Longman, 1988), p. 347.

35. Barbier, *Biographie,* pp. 314–15.

36. Barbier, Frédéric,"L'Industrialisation des techniques," p. 74.

37. AN F18 369. "Aussi la main d'un moine d'autrefois ne pourrait-elle copier en trois ans ce qui se fait en une seule minute dans l'*Imprimerie catholique.*" Migne attributes this quotation to two newspapers, *L'Estafette* and the *Banlieu de Paris;* but in fact, according to Hamman (*Migne,* p. 81), the same phrases also appear on the letterhead of his stationery; and though I have not seen it there, it is entirely possible, for reasons that will become increasingly clear in the section on Migne the publicist that he was entirely capable of having written the newspaper article himself.

38. "The ancients had for a censor their own community; and we, who do we have except for our pride? Nothing they produced was committed to print until it was perfectly finished. Sketches were not allowed to get beyond the walls of the cloister. One was forced, in the phrase of Saint Bernard, to be a reservoir before becoming a canal" (AN F18 1803).

Note that Migne here projects the art of printing back upon a time before its invention. Historical reality was rarely the ultimate criterion of his rhetorical solicitations where selling the patrologies was concerned.

39. *Illustration,* February 22, 1868 (reproduced in Vernet, "Migne," p. 46 and in Hamman, *Migne,* p. 63).

40. L. Marchal reports that "in 1865 he hired forty proofreaders for ten years and under onerous conditions to do the painstaking revision of stereotyped plates" ("Migne," col. 1727). Correction seemed, in fact, one of the ways a worker might earn a little more, for Migne, who insisted on the fact that the five proofreadings to which the patrologies were submitted cost him as much as their setting into type, offered a "bonus" of twenty-five centimes for each error uncovered (Hamman, *Migne,* p. 65).

41. AN F18 333a. See Pierrard, "Migne journaliste," p. 115.

42. Veuillot, Eugène, *Louis Veuillot* (Paris: Victor Retaux, 1899–1913), vol. 1, p. 372.

43. "This numerous body of workers is constantly undergoing transformation, which renders, one must admit, a serious inquiry into the background of each one very difficult for M. l'abbé" (AN F19 5842).

44. Barbier, *Biographie,* p. xxviii.

45. Goncourts, *Journal,* VI, (Monaco, 1956), August 21, 1864, p. 234 (translation mine).

46. See Pierrard, "Migne journaliste," p. 113.

47. "L'ancien desservant y accueille, dès la première heure, nombre de prêtres, les uns, transfuges de la Révolution, les autres venus de la province ou de l'étranger, d'autres enfin, en rupture de ban, mariés et chargés de famille" (Hamman, *Migne,* p. 64).

48. Reproduced in Fouilheron, Joël, "Vu de Saint-Flour. Et s'il était auvergnat?" *Colloque de Saint-Flour,* p. 414.

49. "Tu crois que les Auvergnats d'aujourd'hui valent ceux d'autrefois. . . . Ici à Paris les Auvergnats ne se croient égaux aux autres hommes que quand ils les dépassent en vices" (cited in Fouilheron, "Migne auvergnat?," p. 414).

50. See Pinkney, *Decisive Years,* pp. 151–52.

Chapter 2

1. Barbier, *Biographie,* pp. 307–8. Barbier, who has little distance from his sources, which are rarely specified, here indicates nonetheless that he has obtained knowledge of Migne's *exeat* from the very *Univers religieux* mentioned in it. See also Hamman, *Migne,* p. 57.

2. Pierrard, "Migne journaliste," p. 95. Pierrard's magisterial article on Migne's journalistic activities is to be followed throughout.

3. See Veuillot, Eugène, *Louis Veuillot*, vol. 1, p. 367.

4. Excerpts from this prospectus are reproduced in Pierrard, "Migne journaliste," p. 96. See also Veuillot, *Louis Veuillot*, vol. 1, p. 366.

5. Cited Pierrard, "Migne journaliste," p. 111.

6. Police report of February 1854 (AN F18 333a).

7. See letters of Migne to the Ministre de l'Intérieur of February 7 and 9, 1854. The full title of *La Vérité* ran *A NEWSPAPER FOR MODERATE MEN OF ALL PERSUASIONS. Principles of this Newspaper: Few long articles. The truth of all and in all. Facts not words. Complete impartiality. The whole press in LA VERITE (JOURNAL DES HOMMES MODERES DE TOUTES LES OPINIONS. Bases de ce Journal: Peu de longs articles. La vérité à tous et dans tout. Des faits non des phrases. Impartialité complète. La presse entière dans LA VERITE).*

8. Balzac, Honoré de, *Lost Illusions*, tr. Hunt, Herbert J. (London: Penguin, 1971), pp. 286–87; *Illusions perdues* (Paris: Garnier Frères, 1956), p. 322–23.

9. See Marchal, "Migne," col. 1725–26; Pierrard, "Migne journaliste," pp. 99–101.

10. "My parents," writes Migne, "alarmed over the consequences that such a trial would necessarily have, and seeing, again, my brother without a stable situation, while all the other members of the family were relatively well situated, begged me to desist in my case, and assured me that my brother (to whom I had, by the way, already given 92,000 fr. outright) would henceforth conduct himself properly and would even be able to compensate me fully" (cited in Fouilheron, "Migne auvergnat?" p. 388).

11. See Pierrard, "Migne journaliste," pp. 101–2. The quarrel over ownership of *Le journal des faits* is contained in the long dossier AN F18 369.

12. An internal report of the Ministère de l'Intérieur, Direction de la Sûreté Générale, February 1854, summarizing the difficulties attached to Migne's request for full ownership and direction of *Le journal des faits,* offers an assessment of his general editorial fitness: "The two documents attached to this report show M. l'abbé Migne in the most deplorable light. Thus, he has been condemned for bribery of a postal employee, he has been censured by the Archbishop of Paris for doctrines expressed in *La Vérité,* he is surrounded by suspicious workers. What's more, at the time that M. l'abbé Migne acquired the *Journal des faits,* this paper happened to be under censure for two infractions, a final decision for printing false

news, and another, currently under appeal, for fraudulent reproduction of articles from the *Constitutionnel*. . . . Further, by a ruling handed down on January 27th, the condemnation for fraudulent reproduction of articles was finalized, and the *Journal des faits* now falls under the jurisdiction of article 32 of the organic statute [*décret organique*] which reads as follows: 'Two convictions for wrongdoing or infraction [*délits ou contraventions*] committed within a period of two years will lead to the suppression by law of the newspaper for which the owner or the owners have been convicted'" (AN F18 333a). A memorandum with no date, but which manifestly has been written after the above, concludes: "Recommendation—not to grant the request for an exception, and to execute against the *Journal des faits*, the provision of article 32 of the statute of February 17, 1852 (*legal suppression* [*la suppression de plein droit*])" (AN F18 333a).

13. See Pinkney, *Decisive Years*, p. 72.

14. Martin, Henri-Jean, *Histoire du livre* (Paris: Bibliothèque nationale, 1964). Part II, "Epoque Moderne, XIXe-XXe siècles," pp. 27-28.

15. "The favor requested by l'abbé Migne is one that it is only appropriate to grant in extraordinary circumstances and for the most serious reasons; for it would have the consequence of weakening the effects of the organic statute which furnishes the government with a powerful brake upon the press" (AN F18 333a).

16. In a letter of September 7, 1853, he calls Vassal a "strawman and an ingrate, not to say more" (*un gérant de paille et ingrat pour ne pas dire de plus*). See also notes 19 and 22 of this chapter.

17. "I sense, Monsieur le Directeur, that I must wear you out with all these long letters. I ask a thousand pardons because amongst my motivations is that of informing you and that of protecting the fundamental rights of the family and of society" (AN F18 369).

18. "My rights as a founder of the newspaper, as a creditor and an heir, sacred rights if ever there were any, and which would be completely destroyed and the legal code turned upside down" ("Mes droits de fondateur du Journal, de créancier et d'héritier, droits sacrés s'il en est, se trouvent complètement anéantis et tout le code est bouleversé") (AN F18 369).

19. Letter of August 13, 1853 (AN F18 369). Elsewhere, Migne writes of "A newfangled socialism, armed with a simple legal fiction, and which disappropriates with impunity my property along with a strawman manager who is at bottom nothing and who reduces to nothing he who is in reality all" (AN F18 369).

20. Letter from Montrouge to the Directeur de la Sûreté Générale, December 16, 1853 (AN F18 333a).

21. AN F18 333a. The charge is repeated almost verbatim in a memorandum of February 1854.

22. Thus an internal document of the Ministère de l'Intérieur, Direction de la Sûreté Générale, January 18, 1854: "M. l'abbé Migne is already the managing editor of a newspaper, La Voix de la vérité, and he is disqualified for that reason from being at the same time the managing editor of another newspaper; not only managing editor, but also owner in the name of others, since the laws governing the press makes no distinction between managing editors and editor-in-chief. L'abbé Migne should, then, change his position into that of a chairman of the board [associé commanditaire] and present the other board members as the collective editorial board [et présenter des associés en nom collectifs qui seraient les gérants]. (The one he has presented as manager is only a strawman)" (AN F18 333a). Another from February 1854 comes to the same conclusion: "First of all, M. l'abbé Migne, already managing editor of another newspaper, the Voix de la vérité, cannot at the same time be managing editor of a new newspaper. The co-managing editor he has presented was, in reality, what one calls a strawman, as is shown by the information obtained from the prefecture of police" (AN F18 333a).

23. See Marchal, "Migne," col. 1726; Leterrier, Les Contemporains, no. 21, September 21, 1913, p. 13; Pierrard, "Migne journaliste," pp. 107–8.

24. Cited Pierrard, "Migne journaliste," p. 108. See Leflon, Jean, and Limouzin-Lamothe, R., Mgr Denys-Auguste Affre, archevêque de Paris (Paris: J. Vrin, 1971), pp. 148–50.

25. The report of June 26, 1854, reads: "La Vérité, a newspaper directed and edited by l'abbé Migne, has published for some time now a series of articles under the rubric of The Keeper of the Tomb of Ste Hélène [Le gardien du tombeau de Ste Hélène]. This story, which is more than a little inappropriate [plus que familier] where the life of the First Consul and Emperor Napoleon the First is concerned, contains details so embarrassing [d'une telle inconvenance] for the members of the Imperial family that they border on outrage. The issue of June 25th, among others, is devoted to the marriage of Louis Bonaparte and Hortense de Beaubarnain, which is announced in a very special way. The intent of the writer is flagrant: the imperial reputation [la majesté impériale] is clearly harmed by this miserable libel. Recommendation: to give a warning to the newspaper La Vérité" (AN F18 333a).

26. "Recently I took the key home with me, but at once the mayor

sent his assistant to fetch it with a note he had written himself. It is inconvenient when I have to celebrate a marriage or officiate at a burial to have to travel a long way from the church in order to get this key" (*La Vérité canonique*, t. 2, no. 38, December 21, 1861).

27. *La Vérité canonique*, t. 1, April 6, 1861, pp. 17–18.

28. "A house has been bought for the presbytery, which is now under repair. They have given me possession of the courtyard and a little grazing space for my horse. Well, this grazing area is bordered on the north by the ravine [*ravin*] of a close of trees, elms [*ormeaux*], poplars, etc.

"The commune wants to remove all these trees in order to build a school; it would dispossess me by so doing of benefit of pasture [*des émondes*] and of the protection of a closed-in place" (*La Vérité canonique*, December 21, 1861, p. 361).

29. *La Vérité canonique*, December 21, 1861, p. 362.

30. *La Vérité canonique*, December 21, 1861, p. 364.

31. *La Vérité canonique*, April 6, 1861, pp. 30–31.

32. *La Vérité canonique*, December 21, 1861, pp. 377–78.

33. *La Vérité canonique*, April 6, 1861, p. 31.

34. *La Vérité canonique*, April 6, 1861, p. 32.

35. The caveat at the end of the issue—"*For everything that is not signed:* L. Migne [*Pour tout ce qui n'est pas signé:* L. Migne]" (*sic*)—is, in fact, a little absurd, since almost everything comes from elsewhere.

36. Martin, *Histoire du livre*, p. 32.

37. In the very notion of the absent editor, Migne seems to transform himself into a conducting wire of the truth of others; and we will see how important the image of electricity becomes in his fascination with industrial modernism, and, more specifically, with electricity.

Chapter 3

1. "Je crois rendre à l'Eglise le plus grand service qui lui a jamais été rendu et j'espère bien mourir le prêtre du monde entier qui lui aura fait le plus de bien en ressuscitant intégralement sa tradition" (BN n.a. 24633, fol 478).

2. *Annales de philosophie chrétienne*, 3e série, vol. 14 (1846), pp. 392–93.

3. *Annales de philosophie chrétienne*, 4e série, t. 16, vol. 55 (1857), p. 250.

4. *Annales de philosophie chrétienne*, 5e série, t. 3, vol. 62, (1861), p. 76.

5. The phrase is, moreover, very similar to that also contained in a

review, from the *Annales de philosophie chrétienne,* 3e série, v. 24 (1842), p. 68: "At the time the first prospectuses for this great enterprise appeared, it seemed doubtful that he [the editor] would be able to make good on his promises. Now, doubt is no longer permitted; we have before our eyes more than 80 volumes in-4o." We can further situate the prospectus as having been published before the month of April 1838 in that Migne affirms on page 23 that "Subscribers who sign up before April pay nothing before the end of this month" (AN F18 1803); and on the top of letter-head stationery of a letter written on July 12, 1838, he speaks of, "The PROSPECTUS written and published three months after the distribution throughout the whole of Europe of more than 5,000 letters seeking advice, and after receiving most of the responses."

6. Louis Veuillot will publish his first article in *L'univers religieux* in 1839. For the circumstances of his collaboration, see Veuillot, Eugène, *Louis Veuillot,* vol. 1, p. 175.

7. Miller, Michael B. *The Bon Marché: Bourgeois Culture and the Department Store, 1869–1920* (Princeton: Princeton University Press, 1981), p. 222.

8. English edition, pp. 272–73; French edition, p. 304.

9. Cited in Martin, *Histoire du livre,* p. 34.

10. "From 1816 to 1827, a period when reading rooms, first established for the perusal of newspapers, undertook to supply readers, for a fee, with newly-published books, and when the exorbitant taxes imposed on the periodic press forced it to turn to advertisements, the book-trade had no other means of publicity than articles inserted either in the *feuilletons* or the main text of the newspapers" (*Illusions,* English edition, p. 363; French edition, pp. 410–11).

11. "This means of publicity, restricted first of all to shop-windows and those of the big boulevard establishments, was abandoned in favour of advertisements in the press" (*Illusions,* English edition, p. 363; French edition, p. 411).

12. *Annales de philosophie chrétienne,* 5e série, t. 10, vol. 69 (1864), p. 77.

Chapter 4

1. See Mély, "Migne," p. 219.

2. "I cannot, given the low price of our edition, pay more than 100 francs in cash or 200 francs in books for this work. I know, moreover, that the notes, no matter how few or brief they are, incur an expense for typesetting, correction, stereotyping, paper, impression, smoothing,

binding, and shipping that is so high that I am considering without too much displeasure simply reprinting the Benedictines, if you find yourself unable to accept my offer. I would, however, go as high as 120 francs if you could resist ruining a volume of the Benedictine edition" (BN n. a. 6143, fol. 38).

3. For a fuller list, from which the above partial listing is taken, see Hamman, *Migne,* pp. 107–11; Marchal, "Migne," col. 1732–34; Petitmengin, Pierre, "Les Patrologies avant Migne," in *Colloque de Saint-Flour,* pp. 15–38.

4. Colombet, Claude, *Propriété littéraire et artistique* (Paris: Dalloz, 1980), pp. 6–7; Dock, Marie-Claude, *Etude sur le droit d'auteur* (Paris: Pichon et Durand, 1963), pp. 156–57. The law was further extended in 1854: "First article.—The widows of artists will benefit, for the remainder of their life, from the rights guaranteed by the laws of January 13, 1791, and July 19, 1793, the decree of February 5, 1810, the law of August 3, 1844, and the other laws or decrees concerning this matter.—The length of the benefit accorded to children by these same laws and decrees is extended to thirty years from either the death of the author, composer or artist or the expiration of the rights of the widow" (Worms, Fernand, *Etude sur la propriété littéraire* [Paris: Alphonse Lemerre], p. 360).

5. *Annales de philosophie chrétienne,* 5e série, t. 10, vol. 69, 1864, p. 83.

6. Migne also offers on this page some credit for the critical apparatus, which often blends with an advertisement for it: e.g., for Cyprian: "ET PRAECIPUIS MARTINI ROUTHII, FELLI, PAMELII, RIGALTII LECTIONIBUS ET NOTIS INSTRUCTA, VARIISQUE AUCTA OPUSCULIS RECENTIUS IN LUCEM EDITIS"; for Lactantius: "BUNEMANNI, O. F. FRITZSCHE, N. LE NOURRY CUM EMENDATIONIBUS TUM DISQUITIONIBUS CRITICIS AUCTA"; for Jerome: "SED POTISSIMUM JOANNIS MARTIANAEI HUJUS ORDINIS RECENSIONEM, DENUO AD MANUSCRIPTOS ROMANOS, AMBROSIANOS, VERONENSES ET MULTOS ALIOS, NEC NON AD OMNES EDITIONES GALLICANAS ET EXTERAS CASTIGATA, PLURIMIS ANTEA OMNINO INEDITIS MONUMENTIS, ALIISQUE S. DOCTORIS LUCUBRATIONIBUS SEORSIM TANTUM VULGATIS AUCTA, INNUMERIS NOTIS, OBSERVATIONIBUS, CORRECTIONIBUS ILLUSTRATA STUDIO ET LABORE VALLARSII ET MAFFAEII VERONAE PRESBYTERORUM, OPERAM NAVANTIBUS ALIIS IN EADEM CIVITATE LITTERATIS VIRIS. EDITIO PARISIORUM NOVISSIMA EX SECUNDA AB IPSIS VERONENSIBUS EDITORIBUS CURIS POSTERIORIBUS ITA RECOGNITA, ATQUE EX RECENTIUS DETECTIS SIC DITATA UT PRASENS EDITIO, AMPLITUDINE SOLA, CAETERIS OMISSIS EMENDATIONIBUS, PRAECEDENTES OMNES EDITIONES, ETIAM BENEDICTINAS, *tertia parte seu triente materialiter superet.*"

7. Cited Hamman, *Migne,* p. 132.

8. Cited Hamman, "Principaux collaborateurs des deux Patrologies de Migne," in *Colloque de Saint-Flour,* p. 187.

9. "Your list omits S. Eleutheri ep. Tornacenis sermo. If you do not find it, I will send it to you." Letter of Malou to Migne, February 24, 1844 (cited Hamman, "Principaux collaborateurs," p. 186).

10. Letter cited in Hamman, "Principaux collaborateurs," p. 186.

11. Migne admits to having used the Coustant edition (above, p. 62).

12. Cited Hamman, "Principaux collaborateurs," p. 186.

13. See Hamman, Migne, pp. 78–79.

14. Annales de philosophie chrétienne, 3e série, vol. 20 (1849), p. 316.

15. Dain, Alphonse, Les manuscrits (Paris: Edition "Les Belles Lettres," 1975), p. 181.

16. Dain, Les manuscrits, p. 181; see also Vernet, "Migne," p. 44.

17. Letter of March 11, 1857, cited in Hamman, Migne, p. 77–78.

18. Goncourts, Journal, VI, (Monaco, 1956), August 21, 1864, p. 234.

19. Le R. P. Dom Fernand Cabrol, Histoire du Cardinal Pitra (Paris: Victor Retaux et Fils, 1893), p. 111.

20. Cited Hamman, Migne, p. 124.

21. "I regret more than you the divorce that has taken place between you and M. Migne," Malou writes on November 1, 1861, "and I wish that peace between you could be reestablished on solid ground, at least before the printing of the Conciles!" (cited Hamman, Migne, pp. 123, 125).

22. Cited Hamman, Migne, p. 124.

23. Cited Hamman, Migne, p. 119.

24. Cited Hamman, Migne, p. 129.

25. Prospectus reprinted in Mély, "Migne," p. 213.

26. Annales de philosophie chrétienne, 4e série, t. 16, vol. 55 (1857), p. 247. See also Hamman, Migne, pp. 132–33, and Marchal, "Migne," col. 1731–32.

27. "If we had acted otherwise, we would have limited to certain individuals and to certain countries the good that it is our intention to do. It is a duty, where a work like this one is concerned, to be universal, and, as a result, to fulfill, from beginning to end, the beautiful maxim: In dubiis libertas" (AN F18 1803).

28. Prospectus reprinted in Mély, "Migne," p. 213.

29. Annales de philosophie chrétienne, 4e série, t. 16, vol. 55 (1857), p. 247.

Chapter 5

1. Fouilheron, Joël, "Migne auvergnat?" p. 395.

2. "We [the Delcros] still have ten thousand francs at your disposal, you can make withdrawals without notification . . . and we will find still

more resources if you need them"; "If you can find some easy lender, I am counting on you to do everything possible to find me the money as soon as possible; right now my position is the same as yours after February 1848" (letters cited Fouilheron, "Migne auvergnat?" pp. 389, 391).

3. Letters cited Fouilheron, "Migne auvergnat?" p. 393.

4. See Fouilheron, "Migne auvergnat?" p. 395.

5. See Fouilheron, "Migne auvergnat?" p. 405.

6. "One has not taken sufficient note: our Ateliers catholiques were intentionally founded to produce that which no editor would dare to undertake. What need was there to allow to climb on our back several higher-ups and the mass of booksellers in order to do what one already did without us? What help would we lend to our fellows? What service would we render to the Church? It is the constant and universal exploitation of such a sacred mine that has always revolted us, which has placed arms in our hands and has made us found our work on this double axis: the good at a good price"—"du bon, à bon marché" (*Démonstrations évangéliques*, Paris, 1849, vol. 18, col. 1351).

7. *Annales de philosophie chrétienne*, 3e série, vol. 14 (1846), pp. 393–94. We also find in the *Annales* the following statement: "In order to satisfy this desire and to satisfy it in a useful way, that is to say in such a way as to popularize ecclesiastical learning, and to render it accessible to the class of numerous readers who have not been favored by the gifts of fortune, M. l'abbé Migne wanted not only to reprint the great collections of Catholic science, but also to sell them very cheaply" (*Annales de philosophie chrétienne*, 3e série, vol. 24, 1842, p. 68).

8. "*Cours complets* of the patrology, or complete, uniform, convenient, economical universal Library of all the Holy Fathers, doctors, and ecclesiastical writers who have flourished from the apostles to Innocent III . . . The most careful edition, and superior to all others with respect to the clarity of characters, the quality of the paper, the soundness of the text, the perfection of the correction, the number and variety of volumes reproduced, the uniformity and the usefulness of the format, the low price of the volumes, and particularly with respect to the unified, methodical, chronological collection of six hundred fragments and works from all ages, places and in all languages and forms, up until now scattered here and there, for the first time brought together in our library."

9. See H. Leclercq, "Migne," *Dictionnaire d'archéologie chrétienne*, vol. 1, t. 1, col. 953; Mély, "Migne," pp. 214, 222–23.

10. A propos too of the series of Greek fathers published in Latin:

"For those who are at the same time subscribers to the *Patrologie latine* the price of each volume is .... 5 fr.

"When one only takes the Latin collection of the Greek Fathers, each volume costs............... 6 fr." (*Annales de philosophie chrétienne*, 5e série, t. 14, no. 79, vol. 73 [1866], p. 414).

11. Migne is always concerned about postage and incidental costs: "Outside of France and the Continent, the cost of customs duty and handling charges are extra" (Prospectus of 1838, AN F18 1803). Elsewhere, it seems, certain nations are granted favored trading status: "However, the administration of the *Cours* will itself pay all the costs for the episcopal towns of Holland, Rhenish Prussia, Switzerland, of Bade, of Catalonia, of Navarre and of Savoie, averaging 75 c., for each volume bound, in addition to the usual price, and 50 centimes for Belgium and Corsica" (AN F18 369).

12. AN F118 369. Migne offers exactly the same "avantages" to the subscriber to any twenty volumes not only of the patrologies, but of his other series—the *Encyclopédie théologique*, the *Démonstrations évangéliques*, the *Cours complet d'histoire écclésiastique, Manuel écclésiastique*, etc.: "The subscribers to 20 volumes at once, from among the following list, will benefit, IN FRANCE, from six advantages. . . ." (AN F18 369).

13. *Annales de Philosophie Chrétienne*, 3e série, vol. 14, (1846), p. 393. This offering is, of course, extended not for the original *Cours* of 1838, but the patrologies which begin to appear in 1844.

14. Prospectus in Mély, "Migne," pp. 222-223; See also Marchal, "Migne," col 1727.

15. The price reduction is even greater in a subsequent publication: "Total price of the 2000 volumes for the priest who will subscribe at one time or successively to the whole ....10,000 f.

"Total price of the 2000 for the priest who will pay the whole sum in advance.............7,000 f." (AN F18 369).

16. "Fourteen volumes will have already appeared by that time [April 1838]. Ten more will follow each semester" (AN F18 1803).

17. "Subscribers to only one *Cours* who want to benefit from the six advantages will be obliged to find another subscriber to one of the two *Cours*, without being able to have a right, where this subscriber is concerned, to the first of the *bonuses* which we will set forth. In any case, the subscribers brought in will only benefit from the same right after having, in turn, himself procured a subscriber" (AN F18 1803).

18. *Annales de philosophie chrétienne*, 5e série, t. 10, vol. 69 (1864), p. 82.

19. Prospectus reprinted in Mély, "Migne," p. 213.

20. Prospectus AN F18 1803. Like a traveling salesman, Migne offers a sample of his wares: "Thanks to these precautions, we can guarantee that in spite of the large number of volumes, the large size of the format and that which we just said about them, the material fabrication of the *Cours complets* makes them two exceptional publications, and, so to say, as beautiful on the outside as they are solid from within. The paper of this *Prospectus* is a *sample* of that which is used" (Prospectus, AN F18 1803). In fact, Migne did, where the printing of Greek was concerned, have the engraver Friry create specially a set of roman characters and a set of italic characters, which were used to distinguish citations from the body of the text; and this represented a first in the printing of Greek; see Marchal, "Migne," col. 1732.

21. Cabrol, *Pitra*, p. 112.

22. *Annales de philosophie chrétienne* 3e série, t. 17, (1848), p. 164.

23. Barbier, *Biographie*, p. 315; see also Hamman, *Migne*, p. 61; Leterrier, *Les contemporains*, p. 7.

24. "M. l'abbé Migne is neither the printer nor the bookseller, since the two licenses belong to M. Victor Migne, his brother and his worthy collaborator" (Barbier, *Biographie*, p. 318).

25. Cited Barbier, *Biographie*, p. 320.

26. Marchal, "Migne," col. 1723; Mély, "Migne," pp. 211–12.

27. "I have in my Museums, at excessively moderate prices, magnificent Paintings as well as powerful and excellent Organs; let me recommend their propagation to your spirit of devotion for my work" (Letter to Cardinal Mathieu, cited Hamman, *Migne*, p. 65). See also Vernet, "Migne," pp. 44–45.

28. Fouilheron, "Migne auvergnat?" p. 425.

29. The question of quality is, of course, moot, since none of Migne's artwork has, to my knowledge, been positively identified, though it is quite probable, as the *Moniteur de Cantal* suggests, given the steady traffic in workers, drygoods, and books between Paris and Saint-Flour, that the first place to look for surviving paintings would be in the churches of the region: "Issartier had for some time directed the painting workshops organized in Paris by M. l'abbé Migne, and it is probable that more than one of the churches of our diocese possess one of these productions for whose execution he was responsible" (Cited Fouilheron, "Migne auvergnat?" p. 425). Without identifying his sources, André Vernet asserts that Migne's organs were not manufactured to a very high standard: "An allied commerce in pious objects: paintings, stations of the cross, church ornaments, harmoniums, organs, etc., does not appear to have had much

financial success, in spite of the publicity placed by Migne on the covers of his publications: the praise of great unique organs—of which it must be said in passing that all the parts sooner or later had to be replaced—is in this respect a veritable anthology piece" (Vernet, "Migne," pp. 44–45).

30. Letters cited Fouilheron, "Migne auvergnat?" p. 394.

31. See Vernet, "Migne," pp. 45–46; Leclercq, "Migne," col. 948; Mély, "Migne," p. 225; Trin, Antoine, "La Vie Laborieuse de l'Abbé Migne," *Revue de la Haute-Auvergne,* t. 61 (1959), p. 471.

32. "But does one perhaps fear, following the example of an honorable superior of a seminary, that there might lurk some kind of simony in this proposition? If it were thus, the editors would not have made themselves understood; they are going then to be even more explicit in repeating what they have written to the superior in question: 'The administration of the *Cours complets* accepts the 1000 masses that you have had the goodness to send' " (AN F18 1803).

33. Goncourts, *Journal* VI, p. 234. Migne did, in fact, claim to have the approval of the bishops: "In order to protect sacred things with all imaginable guarantees, we add that, according to our custom, no masses will be distributed except through the proper channels of the secretariat of the bishopric or of the local seminary, or upon our consultation, concerning the applicant, with one of these two organizations" (AN F18 1803).

34. Cited Mély, "Migne," p. 223.

35. English edition, p. 516; French edition, p. 580.

36. Cited Mély, "Migne," p. 223.

37. Prospectus cited in Hamman, *Migne,* p. 80.

38. Reproduced in Mély, "Migne," p. 223; Leclercq, "Migne," col. 948.

39. Should the lender opt, in fact, for this second option, Migne envisions a system of predelivery which corresponds in every way to the prepayment plan outlined elsewhere ("And should they so desire, we are prepared to send them these volumes franco, **right off** and for the **totality** of the interest that will be due them for five full years." The reason for this bonus is, again, one of utility: the volumes owed, like the money lent, should not remain unproductive ("That which has led us to this payment in advance is that the volumes will be of greater use to them installed in their library than piled up in our warehouses; in addition, they will be another guarantee of our good faith"). Leclercq, "Migne," col. 948; Mély, "Migne," p. 224.

40. Mély, "Migne," p. 224.

41. "An unheard-of thing in the heady days of a large operation! Never

in 29 years of extensive business, either by a lapse of memory, or by the negligence of our employees, or by the vengeance of a third party, have we experienced the confusion of a contested bill" (Mély, "Migne," p. 224).

42. "If we do not offer you more than 5%, it is because we have expenses connected to collection, administration, and payment of funds and interest or the mailing of volumes; it is because a borrower who wants to do honor to his affairs and not harm anyone else cannot pay more; it is because the more we offer, the more one should be suspicious of us, for high interest rates stem from great need and the instability of the Institution, in spite of claims to the contrary; finally, it is because fortunate experience has taught us that our Readers do not want to receive any more than the legal rate, anything over that, except where commercial rates are concerned, striking them as canonically and civilly usurious, no matter by what made-up name one calls it" (Mély, "Migne," p. 225).

43. Mély, "Migne," p. 225.

44. Mély, "Migne," p. 223.

45. *Annales de philosophie chrétienne*, 5e série, t. 14, vol. 73 (1866), p. 411.

46. *Annales de philosophie chrétienne*, 5e série, t. 14, vol. 73 (1866), p. 412.

47. *Le Monde illustré*, February 22, 1868, p. 117.

48. *Le Moniteur de Cantal*, February 15, 1868 (cited in Trin, "Migne," p. 470).

49. "In this factory without equal, twelve professions were practiced. Not only did they print books and newspapers there, but they made church organs, holy paintings, statues, bas-reliefs. A great organ worth thirty thousand francs, ready for delivery, was literally melted. At ten o'clock I looked in vain for its trace on the ground covered with smoking embers" (*Le Figaro*, February 13, 1868, p. 1).

50. Migne's vast correspondence was also apparently for the most part preserved. The fact that so few letters written to him survive is due to the fact that Garnier Frères, which bought the Ateliers catholiques after a protracted court battle between Migne and his insurers, sold the envelopes to stamp collectors in keeping with renewed philatelic interest in the 1870s. This may in part be what Hippolyte Garnier meant when he states that "this transaction was the most advantageous he had ever done in his life" (cited in an insert on the abbé Migne by Henri-Jean Martin, *Histoire de d'édition française* [Paris: Bibliothèque nationale, 1964], vol. 3, p. 404).

51. February 15, 1868, p. 25.

52. *Annales de philosophie chrétienne*, 5e série, t. 17, vol. 76 (1868), p. 139.

53. *Annales de philosophie chrétienne*, 5e série, t. 17, vol. 76 (1868), p. 139.

54. Hamman, *Migne*, p. 139.

55. The trial is discussed in Hamman, *Migne*, pp. 137–40; Leclercq, "Migne," col. 956–57; Marchal, "Migne," col. 1725; Vernet, "Migne," pp. 35–36.

56. "The sales of the majority of works were constantly diminishing; thus the *Series of Holy Writings* and that of *Theology* (the two works having benefited from the highest printing, 10,000 copies), started out selling 550 copies on average per year, and have declined most recently to 150 or 200 for the first, and to 100 or 150 for the second" (*Le Droit*, December 22, 1871, p. 879).

57. "The almost complete failure of many works would prevent in any case the costs of stereotyping to be covered, and there would be an infinite advantage in printing in type with moveable characters" (*Le Droit*, December 22, 1871, p. 879).

58. "For certain volumes the demand is so limited that many years might pass before the stock in the warehouse would be exhausted. However, it is clear that under these conditions the insured, acting in consonance with his best interests of course, would begin by printing the works or the volumes which are the most in demand or of which he possesses the smallest quantity, and would only print the others bit by bit as the need arose. And given the fact that he would be paid for all the plates at the same time, he would profit, where a part of the allotted sum is concerned, from interest payments that he would otherwise not have had if the fire had not happened" (*Le Droit*, December 22, 1871, p. 879).

59. *Le Droit*, December 22, 1871, p. 879.

60. *Le Droit*, December 22, 1871, p. 879.

61. *Annales de philosophie chrétienne*, 5e série, t. 17, vol. 76 (1868), p. 141.

62. "The only thing remaining was three sheets of the last *six volumes*, containing *240 general and specific tables*, in particular an *Index rerum* indicating all the subjects treated by each Father of the Church, an *Index Scripturae sacrae* indicating by which Fathers and in which part of their works each verse of holy scripture has been the object of commentary, from the first verse of *Genesis* to the last of the *Apocalypse*. The *first five volumes of these tables* had been printed; but no one had time to bind the last, that is to say, volume 223 of the whole collection, the sixth of the

general table, which alone cost two years of typographic work. The plates were destroyed, one fears even that the proofs and the manuscript burned, which means that it will be necessary to begin again, as if nothing had yet been done" (*Annales de philosophie chrétienne,* 5e série, t. 17, vol. 76 [1868], p. 141).

63. *Annales de philosophie chrétienne,* 5e série, t. 17, vol. 76 (1868), p. 143.

64. *Annales de philosophie chrétienne,* 5e série, t. 17, vol. 76 (1868), p. 143.

65. "The pretense of wanting to estimate the mercenary value of a work of this type does not seem acceptable to me. When a Company insures commercial establishments containing merchandise with a market price, like wheat, flour, cotton, wool or other goods whose price fluctuates, it is easy to estimate such values, but this is not at all the case for this collection *sui generis*" (*Le Droit,* December 22, 1871, p. 879).

Conclusion

1. English edition, p. 107; French edition, p. 114–15.

2. Balzac attributes the invention of vellum paper to Ambroise Didot ("The invention of vellum paper by Ambroise Didot only dates from 1780" [*Illusions,* English edition, p. 109; French edition, p. 118]), while it was in fact developed by the English printer Baskerville around 1750; see Audin, Maurice, Introduction to Martin, *Histoire du livre,* p. ii.

3. "Formerly, in order to bond the paper, one dipped the sheets in a weak, hot gelatin solution. One stretched them out on drying racks, then one took them to press in order to give them a form. Now one bonds them in the vat itself. For that one mixes in resin cake, gelatin and alum, or wax soap, starch and alum" (Duckett, William, *Le Dictionnaire de la conversation et de la lecture* [Paris: Belin-Mandar, 1837], vol xliii, article entitled "Papier"). The question of mixing the paper is discussed at length in the third section of *Illusions perdues.*

4. See Moran, James, *Printing Presses: History and Development from the 15th Century to Modern Times* (Berkeley: University of California Press, 1978), pp. 41–43; Audin, Introduction to Martin, *Histoire du livre,* p. vii.

5. See Audin, Maurice, *Histoire de l'imprimerie. Radioscopie d'une ère: de Gutenberg à l'informatique* (Paris: A. and J. Picard, 1972), p. 248; Audin, Introduction to Martin, *Histoire du livre,* p. viii; Moran, *Printing Presses,* pp. 101-109.

6. Cited Moran, *Printing Presses,* p. 129.

7. See Moran, *Printing Presses,* p. 140.

8. See Audin, Introduction to Martin, *Histoire du livre,* p. viii; Martin, *Histoire du livre,* p. 79; Moran, *Printing Presses,* p. 129.

9. English edition, p. 491–92; French edition, p. 553.

10. See Barbier, "L'industrialisation des techniques," p. 72; Martin, *Histoire du livre,* pp. 72–79.

11. English edition, p. 18; French edition, p. 21.

12. See Martin, *Histoire du livre,* p. 81; on the term "library" used in the sense of a collection, see Chartier, Roger, *L'ordre des livres: lecteurs, auteurs, bibliothèques en Europe entre le XIVe et le XVIIIe siècles* (Aix-en-Provence: Alinea, 1992), chap. 3.

13. Pinkney, *Decisive Years,* p. 23. "From almost every point of view, therefore, 1840 seems to have been a major turning point for French industry, and whatever 'revolution' it may have experienced was nurtured in the later years of the July Monarchy and came to full bloom in the '50s" (Johnson, Christopher H., "The Revolution of 1830 in French Economic History," in *1830 in France,* ed. Merriman, John M. [New York: New Viewpoints, 1975], p. 147).

14. Crouzet, François, "French Economic Growth in the Nineteenth Century Reconsidered," *History* 59 (1974): p. 170. See also Crouzet, "Essai de construction d'un indice de la production industrielle au XIXe siècle," *Annales ESC* 25 (1970): pp. 56–99; Johnson, Christopher H., "The Revolution of 1830 in French Economic History," pp. 139–89; Lévy-Leboyer, Maurice, "Innovations and Business Strategies in Nineteenth- and Twentieth-century France," in *Enterprise and Entrepreneurs in Nineteenth- and Twentieth-Century France,* ed. Carter, Edward C., Forster, Robert, and Moody, Joseph (Baltimore: Johns Hopkins University Press, 1976), pp. 87–136.

15. As Lévy-Leboyer has shown, rural buying power increased sharply in the period 1835–45; see "La croissance économique en France au XIXe siècle. Résultats préliminaires," *Annales ESC* 23 (1968): pp. 778–807. Jean-Charles Asselain claims that the annual rate of growth in the half century in question was 1.2 percent, a figure not surpassed until after World War II (*Histoire économique de la France du XVIIIe siècle à nos jours* [Paris: Seuil, 1984], p. 139).

16. See Pinkney, *The Decisive Years,* p. 10; Asselin, *Histoire économique,* p. 147.

17. See Miller, *The Bon Marché,* pp. 19–47.

18. Cited in Miller, *The Bon Marché,* p. 26. The actual prospectus is to be found in the Bibliothèque nationale, 4 WZ3230.

19. For a discussion of this tension where the *magasins de nouveauté* are concerned, see Miller, *The Bon Marché,* chapter 6.

20. Miller, *The Bon Marché,* p. 25; Pinkney, *Decisive Years,* p. 48.

21. As Michael Miller notes, even though they were regarded by smaller merchants as a threatening breed apart, the *magasins de nouveauté* were until somewhat later still essentially drygoods emporia (*The Bon Marché,* p. 25).

22. Miller, *The Bon Marché,* p. 99.

23. Zola, Emile, *Au bonheur des dames* (Paris: Garnier-Flammarion, 1971), p. 258 (translation mine).

❖ INDEX OF NAMES

150   Index of Names

❖ SUBJECT INDEX

151